# Imagination,

*Imagination, Illness and Injury* examines the psychological factors behind perceptual limitations and distortions and links a broad range of somatic manifestations with their resolution.

Melanie Starr Costello applies Jungian theory to a variety of cases, attributing psychosomatic phenomena to cognitive processes that are common to us all. She analyses the role of illness in several life narratives, and interprets the appearance of somatic phenomena during important phases of analytic treatment. Together these case narratives present a significant challenge to established views of psychosomatics. Subjects covered include:

- archetypal constrictions of identity
- somatic elements of perception
- the psyche-soma split

*Imagination, Illness and Injury* brings a fresh perspective to the understanding and treatment of the psychotherapy client as a psychosomatic unity. Jungian analysts, psychoanalysts, and psychotherapists will greatly benefit from the clinical applications of archetypal theory presented here.

**Melanie Starr Costello** is a Jungian Analyst in private practice in Washington, D.C. She is a graduate of the C.G. Jung Institute-Zürich and holds a PhD in the History and Literature of Religions from Northwestern University. She lectures frequently in the United States on the topic of psychology and spirituality.

# Imagination, Illness and Injury

## Jungian psychology and the somatic dimensions of perception

Melanie Starr Costello

 Routledge
Taylor & Francis Group

LONDON AND NEW YORK

First published 2006 by Routledge
27 Church Road, Hove, East Sussex BN3 2FA

Simultaneously published in the USA and Canada
by Routledge
270 Madison Avenue, New York, NY 10016

*Routledge is an imprint of the Taylor & Francis Group, an informa
business*

Typeset in Sabon by RefineCatch Limited, Bungay, Suffolk
Printed and bound in Great Britain by
TJ International Ltd, Padstow, Cornwall
Paperback cover design by Sandra Heath

*British Library Cataloguing in Publication Data*
A catalogue record for this book is available from the British Library

*Library of Congress Cataloging-in-Publication Data*
Costello, Melanie Starr.
   Imagination, illness and injury: Jungian psychology and the somatic
dimensions of perception / Melanie Starr Costello.
      p. cm.
   Includes bibliographical references and index.
   ISBN13: 978-0-415-37637-2 (hbk)
   ISBN10: 0-415-37637-8 (hbk)
   ISBN13: 978-0-415-37638-9 (pbk)
   ISBN10: 0-415-37638-6 (pbk)
   1. Psychological manifestations of general diseases.   2. Jungian
psychology.   3. Perception.   I. Title.
   [DNLM: 1. Jungian Theory.   2. Perception.   3. Somatosensory
Disorders.   WM 460.5.J9 C841i 2006]
RC49.C673 2006
616.001'9—dc22                                      2006009408

ISBN10: 0-415-37637-8 (hbk)
ISBN10: 0-415-37638-6 (pbk)

ISBN13: 978-0-415-37637-2 (hbk)
ISBN13: 978-0-415-37638-9 (pbk)

For Margaret

# Contents

# Acknowledgements

I am forever grateful to my friends, colleagues, and especially to my analysands who have nurtured my imagining of the psyche-soma. An immeasurable debt of gratitude goes to those individuals who allowed me to include their stories in this work.

I thank the Susan Bach Foundation for the grant that supported the initial stage of research for this project. I am also grateful to Kate Hawes, Dawn Harris and Claire Lipscomb at Routledge for their hard work and patient help with manuscript preparation.

Without the collegial encouragement and loving support of Phyllis Blakemore LaPlante, Polly Armstrong, Julie Bondanza and Mary Ayers, this book would not have come to completion. My gratitude to you is indelibly attached to the memory of this process.

Finally, my love and heartfelt thanks to Marianne Vysma and Cedrus Monte. Your companionship remains the most meaningful part of the journey.

# Introduction

This book is written for individuals interested in the relationship between somatic phenomena and insight in psychotherapy. It investigates the interplay between body and psyche in the synthesis and contextualization of experience. As an aid to clinicians, the study offers a practical and conceptual frame for working with disturbances in reality perception, common to even the most functional persons who submit themselves to treatment.

The study explores behavioral and somatic dimensions of a condition referred to as "knowing-and-not-knowing." When knowing-and-not-knowing, an individual has not fully apprehended an experience. It is a borderland of consciousness, where experience is registered in some form, but only diffusely thought, if thought at all. In our analysis of cases, states of anxiety, compulsions, dysfunctional behavioral or relational patterns, along with other neurotic and somatic symptoms, are portrayed as expressions of knowledge that has not been adequately represented to consciousness.

In its focus upon cognition in relation to somatic image, sensation, bodily injury and illness, the study joins the psychoanalytic dialogue on psychosomatics. But while most studies on the topic aim toward detection of underlying psychopathology, the present work grew out of the discovery of somatic presentations in conjunction with the *resolution* of psychic conflict.

In my early work as a Jungian analyst I observed a pattern where heightened sensation, injury or illness often preceded the emergence of insight or the resolution of perceptual distortions among my analysands. This engendered my interest in the relationship between somatic experience and the perceptual process, particularly in connection with that state of consciousness where something is both known and not known. Through analysis of cases presented in this study, I have come to view "knowing-and-not-knowing" as a state of somatic pre-consciousness.

Of course, knowing-and-not-knowing states of consciousness among victims of massive trauma have long been of interest in psychiatry. Automatisms, amnesias, and other dissociative behaviors are ways in which the psyche expresses experiences that are too painful for integration into memory. As trauma specialists observe, it is in the nature of trauma to elude knowledge because trauma threatens psychic integrity. Still, knowing occurs on some level, often in restricted forms.

Forms of knowing-and-not-knowing in trauma victims cover a broad spectrum, ranging from severe dissociative states to more integrated and subjectively owned levels of knowing. In severe cases, memory may be warded off by primitive mechanisms of defense such as denial, splitting, amnesia, derealization and depersonalization. Other forms of knowing may manifest via fugue states where the traumatic event is periodically relived but kept separate from the conscious self. In less dissociative forms of knowing, the trauma victim may express the traumatic memory through transference phenomena. Isolated fragments of repressed traumatic memories then impinge upon one's perceptions in the present, influencing the victim's experience of life situations (Laub and Auerhahn 1993).

Where trauma comprises the primary topic of inquiry, somatic manifestations will naturally be viewed in terms of defense against unbearable affect and memory. For example, Don Kalshed's important work on archetypal defenses of traumatized patients views somatization as a defensive division of experience into mental and somatic poles of the unconscious. This polarization protects one from unbearable psychic pain by preventing mental representation of bodily impulses and feelings (Kalshed 1996: 66–7).

But what of those cases of knowing-and-not-knowing that are not directly attributable to massive trauma? What of those moments common to us all when a diffuse feeling translates into an insight and we find ourselves saying "I knew it all along! I knew, but I didn't know!" Are all such instances attributable to the same mechanisms of repression, dissociation, and denial as we find in cases of trauma? Do they involve distortions of memory, as does trauma?

After observing many instances of knowing-and-not-knowing among non-traumatized associates and analysands, several motifs came into view. Instances typically centered upon important, often difficult, life issues. Most cases involved *distortions of perception rather than inhibitions of memory*. Within the analytic frame, I noticed a temporal connection between somatic disturbance – accident, injury, heightened sensation or illness – and the resolution of perceptual distortions.

To flesh out the dynamics involved, I selected a number of cases for further study and, where possible, interviewed the individuals involved. Because knowing-and-not-knowing phenomena are inextricably linked with intrapsychic factors, I concentrated largely upon narratives offered by analysands whose inner lives I had come to know well. Also included in the present work are two striking non-analytic examples: an examination of Albert Speer's relationship with Hitler, based upon historical biography; and a case of child neglect, based upon a life narrative recounted through interview.

The cases selected demonstrate a broad range of knowing-and-not-knowing phenomena. Together they point to an unconscious counterforce to the faculty of the will. Under the diverse conditions presented in our case examples, this "shadow of the will" prohibits the synthesis of selected fragments of experience – internal as well as external – into meaningful constructs (perceptions), effecting a reversion to perceptual functions characteristic of early childhood. As a result, one's breadth of perspective is dramatically narrowed, so that what *could* be seen is not *cognitively* apprehended. Instead, the seen-but-not-perceived content may be held in a borderland between unconscious and conscious fields, leaving the subject in a twilight state of knowing.

This borderland *appears to be the body*, functioning as a repository for fragments of experience withheld from the field of consciousness. The hypothesis of soma as a repository for such fragments is inferred by the observation of *somatic expressions of knowledge* – via smell, injury, or in psychosomatic symptoms. In these instances, knowing is held and expressed through the body until "soma presentations" are attached to a coherent complex. Before this can happen, an associative bridge must be constructed, either by psychotherapeutic means or through life experience.

While the phenomenon of knowing-and-not-knowing concerns ego integrity and defense and bears many similarities to repression and its effects, it is to be distinguished from repression as classically defined. Repression entails the *exclusion* of something from conscious memory that was once perceived, or partly perceived (Freud's "mental act"); the cases examined in this study point to a *disruption in perception itself*. I attribute this disruption to either of two intrapsychic forces: (1) the prolonged influence of an archetype upon an individual's identity or (2) the effects of "complex fragments" from the personal unconscious, the contents of which have never been represented to consciousness.

In concert with other authors I consider the unobstructed continuum of somatic to psychic experiencing the basis of healthy mental, emotional and symbolic functioning. However, I go against conventional wisdom by placing certain psychosomatic phenomena in a progressive (vs. regressive) frame and by emphasizing structural over defense operations. In my view, the focus on trauma and child abuse in psychotherapy (what James Hillman 1997 considers our entrenchment in the child archetype) temps us to automatically attribute psychosomatics to deficient mothering, developmental injury and trauma without considering more commonplace influences such as identity, archetypal functions, and the complexes. By spotlighting the role of archetype and complex in the analysis of cases, I hope to redress the imbalance. To this end, I will be in dialogue with psychoanalytic tradition and object relations theorists as well as Jungian authors.

While Analytical Psychology (the Jung school of psychoanalysis) has paid scarce attention to psychosomatics, works by Mira Sidoli (2000) and Denise Gimenez Ramos (2004), published subsequent to my initial draft, have helped me to expand my imagining of archetypal activity in the body. Some points of difference bear mentioning.

Sidoli, in concert with psychoanalyst Joyce McDougall (1989), traces psychosomatic phenomena back to problems of affect regulation in infancy due to impaired mother–infant relations. For Sidoli, somatization signifies the entrapment of unconscious affect in the body. She believes this affect is *always* pre-Oedipal and belongs to the collective shadow – the primitive archetypal affects of early infancy. In my view, somatization covers a broader and less systematic spectrum than Sidoli has it. As we will see, somatic forms of knowing may be determined by archetypal constellations activated in childhood, adolescence or later in life. And while the body may indeed harbor primitive affect, elements of personal shadow (Oedipal and post-Oedipal contents) also express themselves somatically. Indeed, personal shadow contents often pass into consciousness in conjunction with somatic presentations.

This study also covers new ground in its emphasis on perception and the role of the archetypes in *limiting* as well as fostering the symbolization of experience. In so doing, I investigate aspects of archetypal functioning falling outside the scope of Ramos' important book, *The Psyche of the Body* (2004). Ramos views psychosomatics through a Jungian lens, focusing upon symbolic representations held in the body by means of repression. Some case studies in this book cover this territory. However, my work primarily concerns the perceptual borderland, where experience is *partly* registered but not fully symbolized. Such knowing-and-not-knowing occurrences fall outside the parameters of repression and are commonly experienced. As will be shown, analysis of this psychosomatic "borderland" is key to the advancement of the basic functions of cognitive discernment, resolution of repetitive behaviors, and authentic identity formation.

Insofar as they are linked with the unrepressed unconscious, knowing-and-not-knowing states bear some similarity to what object relations analyst Christopher Bollas calls the "unthought known." Bollas observes the means by which patients use the analyst as an unconscious object, expressing through the transference aspects of their early object relations that have not been mentally represented. Thus the "unthought known" signifies assumptions in relational dynamics that are felt and acted upon without being "mentally processed accurately" (Bollas 1987: 280). I view such unrepressed contents of the unconscious as somatically expressed complex-fragments. Exceeding the developmental parameters of an object relations approach, this study portrays complex-fragments as undigested experiences registered by the soma throughout the life cycle. As detailed in Chapter 4, these unrepressed fragments of perception may achieve representation through analytic work. Our case demonstrates how dream analysis and associative linking fosters the coalescence of somatically harbored percepts into coherent, conscious "feeling-toned complexes."

To set the stage for analysis of specific cases of knowing-and-not-knowing, a general summary of traditional Freudian and Jungian views of perception comprises Chapter 1. There Jung's work on the "feeling-toned complex" is presented as the point of divergence from Freud's systematic portrait of psyche most relevant to our topic. In reviewing early theoretical differences between the founders of the two schools, I wish to underscore the continuing value of complex theory for illumining opaque areas of human behavior.

The case narratives presented in this study are grouped thematic-
ally. Part 1 emphasizes the role of complex and archetype in
knowing-and-not-knowing states of consciousness. Chapters 2 and
3 feature individuals suffering deficits in their ability to synthesize
key factors in their environment. We trace cognitive inhibition in
both cases to archetypal constructs that dominate the individual's
perceptions of self and other. In such cases, areas of experience
standing outside these dominant archetypal constructs are nonetheless registered and expressed somatically: in the first case, by means
of injury; in the second, in illness. Chapter 4 links perceptual
inhibition with the repetition compulsion. Treating an instance of
repetition as a knowing-and-not-knowing phenomenon, we are able
to link the compulsion to activated complex-fragments – percepts
striving for inclusion into a coherent feeling-toned-complex.

Part 2 places the somatic dimensions of perception against the
backdrop of the interpersonal origins of consciousness. In Chapters 6
and 7, two cases of lifelong psychosomatic suffering portray the
body as a perceptual field that registers internal and external sensations that have not attained mental representation. These individuals
suffer impaired judgment as the result of deficiencies in archetypal
constellations during infancy. The final case study as presented
in Chapter 8 reviews an analysand's effort to repair deficiencies
in the maternal *imago* through body representations in painting.
Her picture series portrays the intimate connection between the
body field of knowing, the child archetype, and childhood modes
of perception.

Analytic work always concerns the translation of the unknown
but present self into the fullness of identity. Thus it remains the
best possible context for repair and development of the perceptual
system. Despite its undeniable centrality, the role of the body
in analysis just begins to gain our collective attention. While a
comprehensive presentation of analytic approaches to the somatic
pre-conscious falls outside the parameters of this study, I hope this
analysis of cases contributes in some measure to our growing
apperception of psyche-soma unity. I am indebted to those who, by
offering their stories for this study, awakened me to soma as the
ground of all imagining.

# Part I

# Chapter I

# The imaginal system
## Archetypes and complexes as perceptual determinants

Human consciousness is the great mystery of creation. The means by which we apprehend inner life and outer world have mystified philosophers and scientists for centuries. Learned dialogues on the nature of consciousness often return to one key question: is it possible to perceive the world as it truly is? From the founding fathers of psychoanalysis we have inherited many assumptions about reality perception originating in nineteenth-century philosophy and science. Of particular influence on both Freud and Jung was the Kantian view of perception as subjectively conditioned. This axiom continues its hold on psychoanalytic imagination: we do not regard what is perceived in consciousness as identical with the object, whether that object is physical or psychical. Unconscious mental products are the true objects of our perceptions.

In common parlance, *perception* refers to the mental apprehension of sensation or experience. The Latin word *percipere* denotes the taking of something (*capere*) through (*per*), that is, to thoroughly take up something. To know an experience, percepts from the various modalities – hearing, seeing, touching, along with proprioceptive sensations – must first be *perceived*, then *apperceived* (contextualized and given meaning), and finally formulated at the cognitive level.

We may therefore speak of a hierarchy of perceptual functioning. The hierarchy begins with those sensory processes known to both humans and animals and ascends to the highly complex levels of verbal and pictorial formulations that are distinctively human. Those processes that mark the province of human knowing involve the elaboration of experience in the fullness of meaning.

In imagining a hierarchy of perceptual experience, psychoanalyst David Beres' (1960) model of perceptive functioning is particularly helpful. Beres speaks of three levels of perceptive experience: the pre-perceptual level; the level of percept; the level of imagination. The rudimentary level is the *pre-perceptual*. Pre-perceptual experience involves sense data from the primary modalities. This includes the responses of the sensory nerve endings to temperature, pain, touch, proprioception, and pressure. Also included are the special sensory responses of vision, hearing, taste and smell. At this level of experience we speak of *sensation*, signifying a neuro-physiological experience that is non-reflective.

At the next level primary sensations are organized into *percepts*. Percepts, found in human and animal mentation, are characterized by their relation to direct and immediate sensory stimulation. They are gestalts and configurations of space, form, and color and are recognizable by the responses they produce. Percepts may involve complicated mentation, but at this level the imaginative process has not come into play. This level of organization of experience involves *signals* rather than mental representations, or images.

The level of perception that is characteristically human is the level to which Beres applies the term *imagination*. Here percepts are organized with the involvement of a number of ego functions, producing *mental representations*. Perception achieves representation independent of immediate and direct sensory stimulation. At this level,

> Stimuli emanating from the outer world are organized into a concept of this outer world, of reality; and stimuli emanating from the body organs and the muscles contribute to another part of the concept of reality, the image of the self. But in both instances the stimuli must pass through a complex process before they are conceptualized in the mind.
>
> (Beres 1960: 328)

The distance between the first two levels of perception and the third level is, of course, tremendous. At the first two levels perception is physiological; while at the third, we experience psychic perception, involving mental representation of external and internal reality. Only through the employment of mental representation, that is of imagination, are percepts transformed into perceptions. *Apperception* – the process whereby we contextualize experience – presupposes this transposition of physiological experience into psychic perception. From this activity of abstraction and conceptualization of sensory experience follows *cognition*, the apprehension of what is apperceived into the fullness of understanding (Beres 1960: 327–34).

This complex movement from physiological perception to psychic perception is, of course, subjectively conditioned. The awareness we bring to experience involves intricate connections between event, memory, meaning, interpretation, and character. Perceptions draw upon and add to a repertoire of life experience; as apperceptions they have been arranged and colored by our individuality. Our memories and personal identities are a matrix in which experience is contextualized and meaningfully elaborated.

Without imagination, reality cannot be experienced reflectively. With imagination, reality attains representation, becoming an object of consciousness. The mystery of imagining as the means by which we experience the world is the motive force of Jung's psychology:

> Far too little in theory, and almost never in practice, do we remember that consciousness has no direct relation to any material objects. We perceive nothing but images, transmitted to use indirectly by a complicated nervous apparatus. Between the nerve-endings of the sense-organs and the image that appears in consciousness, there is interpolated an unconscious process which transforms the physical fact of light, for example, into the psychic image "light." But for this complicated and unconscious process of transformation consciousness could not perceive anything material.
>
> (Jung 1933: 383–4)

The various depth psychologies recognize the products of our imagining – words, ideas, pictorial imagery, even spacial elaborations – as conditioned by cultural and individual factors. But Analytical Psychology further distinguishes this conditioning from the enduring, ubiquitous structural element: the archetypal pattern.

Where classical psychoanalysis attributes the *organization* of percepts to the ego's reality functions, Analytical Psychology attributes perception largely to the formal operations of the archetypes. As is well known, Jung conceived his model of the psyche by observing the *effects* of unconscious processes upon consciousness. Among the effects that he observed was the uniformity and regularity of human perceptions regardless of the boundaries of time and culture. Universal themes in myth, folk tales and dreams suggested a transcultural and transpersonal point of origination. Jung called the apparatuses determining our *modes* of apprehension the "archetypes" and he envisioned them as the contents of the "collective unconscious." Thus he conceived the collective unconscious as something that developed out of humanity's experience of the world over the course of eons. As elements that have "crystallized out" of that world, the archetypes function as "ruling powers" determining our modes of perception and our instinctive responses (Jung 1943: 95).

Our apprehension of experience is structured by these innate archetypal forms and, in response to these forms, consciousness reaches out into the environment in search of corresponding elements. But the way in which experience is selected, colored, and contextualized will be influenced by factors unique to the individual.

The dynamic interplay between archetypal factors and individual qualities begins in infancy. An experience acquires a positive or negative quality, depending upon the infant's success in finding correspondences between archetypal forms and environmental features. The general valence of these positive and negative correspondences is an essential factor determining strengths and weaknesses, response and defense patterns, reality functions, and organizational capacities of the ego complex.

Archetypes determine our perceptions of both the external world and of inner drives and mediate them to consciousness by means of mental representations (images). This formulation begs a question: if archetypes are unconscious determinants of images that appear in consciousness, does the ego not have a role in image production? *Where* in the psychic system is the image itself formed? In the conscious? The unconscious? Jung himself would have objected to the question; he rejected psychoanalytic attributions of dynamic processes to functions located in distinct systems, suggesting instead that we "accustom ourselves to the thought that conscious and unconscious have no clear demarcations, the one beginning where the other leaves off" (Jung 1954: 200). For example, contents of the personal unconscious are perfectly conscious in certain respects but are known to a subject only "under a particular aspect" or at a particular time (Jung 1935: 57).

> Freud is seeing the mental processes as static, while I speak in terms of dynamics and relationship. To me all is relative. There is nothing definitely unconscious; it is only not present to

the conscious mind under a certain light. You can have very different ideas of why a thing is known under one aspect and not known under another aspect. The only exception I make is the mythological pattern, which is profoundly unconscious, as I can prove by the facts.

(Jung 1935: 62–3)

Even while accepting the relativity of the unconscious to consciousness, we cannot help but depend upon temporal and spacial analogies for our imagining of body, archetype, and identity as determinants in the dynamics of perception. And as Jung himself admits, archetypal components of psyche remain forever unconscious to us, that is, they reside *in* the unconscious. As unconscious perceptual determinants residing outside the ego-complex, archetypes can never be accessed in themselves by consciousness (Jung 1954: 213–14). We must therefore picture the unconscious, rather than the ego-complex, as the "place" where archetypal operations transform sensory impressions into meaningful constructs. Thus, the mental representation (image) is something that stands between the archetype as the formal unconscious element in perception and the consciousness that apprehends it. At the same time, it becomes necessary to speak of mental representations as "appearing at" (or "over") the threshold of ego-consciousness, for all representations, even highly typical motifs, must contain *conscious* personal elements before consciousness can apprehend them (Jacobi 1959: 35).

It also follows that the archetype is the agent responsible for the selection and synthesis of personal contents for the production of mental representations. And we must assume the involvement of the *personal unconscious* when we consider the necessary mingling of percepts with existing elements of experience (memories, emotions, ideas) – personal elements that rest for the most part in the unconscious until archetypal operations release them into consciousness. Perhaps Jung had this function in mind when he speaks of the "*archetypes* of perception and apprehension, which are the necessary *a priori* determinants of all psychic processes" (Jung 1948a: 133).

Perceptions become available to consciousness through a complex process of selection, categorization, and synthesis of stimuli. Attributing these functions to archetypal operations, we depart radically from the Freudian tradition, which assigns these synthetic functions to the ego as the seat of judgment and intelligence. Where Freudian psychology views the ego as a medial function, regulating the intake of external stimuli and organizing internal responses (originating from the "id"; Freud 1923: 18–39), Analytical Psychology conceives the ego as but one among myriad complexes, a feeling-toned group of representations of oneself whose nature is both conscious and unconscious. Analytical Psychology places the ego at the center of consciousness, but it is not considered the psyche's center.

While Jung characteristically emphasizes the role of archetypes in perception, he attributes to the ego-complex the determination of *how* a mental representation is apperceived. In his (1931) essay entitled "The Structure of the Psyche," Jung makes the distinction between *sense perception* as a physiological process, and *apperception* as a complex psychic process. In apperception, four functions of consciousness interplay. The thing perceived by the senses first becomes recognizable through *thinking*. Memory images will be utilized in the course of recognition to which the perceived thing will be compared and differentiated. Then, the recognized thing will be evaluated in accordance with the *feeling-tone* associated with that recognition; this will be influenced by the emotional phenomena attached to the memory-images utilized. *Intuition* may also come into play in apperceiving something, should the experience elicit insight into the possibilities inherent in a situation. These faculties of apperception – thinking, feeling, sensation, and intuition – stand among the basic components that shape one's individuality. The strengths and weaknesses of these functions in any given individual (a person's typology) contribute to the many features of personality which lend uniqueness to that person's way of experiencing self and world.

The four functions of consciousness denote apperception as a rational process directed by attention (a quantum of psychic energy available to the ego). Nonetheless, irrational and undirected apperception may be found in dreaming and fantasy, which Jung includes in the category of consciousness "because they are the most important and most obvious results of unconscious psychic processes obtruding themselves upon consciousness" (Jung 1931: 140–2).

Jung's reflections on subliminal forms of perception make apparent how far he deviated from the Freudian emphasis upon perception as an ego function. Jung believed mental representations may, under certain circumstances, be perceived *in* the unconscious, exclusive of consciousness. Since we cannot know the unconscious in itself, he notes, we cannot exclude the possibility that the unconscious may contain the very functions which we attribute to consciousness – including perception, apperception, memory, imagination, will, affectivity, feeling, reflection, and judgment.

> The hypothesis of the threshold and of the unconscious means that the indispensable raw material of all knowledge – namely psychic reactions – and perhaps even unconscious "thoughts" and "insights" lie close beside, above, or below consciousness, separated from us by the merest "threshold" and yet apparently unattainable. We have no knowledge of how this unconscious functions, but since it is conjectured to be a psychic system it may possibly have everything that consciousness has, including perception, apperception, memory, imagination, will, affectivity, feeling, reflection, judgment, etc., all in subliminal form.
>
> (Jung 1954: 171–2)

To the objection that one cannot possibly speak of *unconscious* perceptions or images because these can only be represented to an experiencing subject, Jung retorts, "the psychic process remains essentially the same whether it is 'represented' or not" (Jung 1954: 172). In a similar context Jung points out that in the symptomatology of somnambulism and other pathologies where consciousness is morbidly restricted, we observe unconscious processes that bear the marks of *conscious* processes:

> One can only say that these people perceive, think, feel, remember, decide, and act unconsciously, doing unconsciously what others do consciously. These processes occur regardless of whether consciousness registers them or not.
>
> (Jung 1931: 143)

Jung's observations led him to muse upon the possibility that the complexes of the unconscious represent in themselves "splinter psyches." We will return to this issue as we observe "somatic" forms of perception in Chapters 4, 5, and 6. There we consider the body as a perceiving "subject" in itself.

## The ego and the feeling-toned-complex: perceptual distortions and omissions

Our exploration of the perceptual process stems from our imaging of the dynamic interplay of psychic forces. Since Analytical Psychology departs from Freudian tradition in its portrait of psychic structure, our approach to the problem of reality perception is also distinctive.

Classical psychoanalytic theory is fashioned out of the discovery of conflict between psychic systems. It therefore views those processes by which the mind apprehends itself and the world with regard to ego defense mechanisms observed in psychopathology. Inquiry into the perceptual system is weighted toward the problem of memory – the mind's retention and recollection of affective and sensory experience. Freud's momentous discovery was of the process whereby certain perceptions and impulses may be ejected from ego-consciousness and subsequently retained in an unconscious system – the ego's defense operation called *repression*.

In psychoanalytic theory, repressed contents make themselves known in various ways. An objectionable impulse, severed by the process of repression from the ideas and conceptions that give meaning to its aim, retains its energic charge and seeks outlets. This activity produces "derivatives," fragments of perception that attach themselves to associated but less objectionable ideas available to consciousness. These *remnants of perception* – memory traces – reside, so to speak, within the ego and comprise the system which Freud named the "preconscious" (Freud 1915b: 180–5). In psychoanalytic practice the patient's attention is drawn to these derivates with a view to encouraging the process whereby repressed contents become preconscious by regaining verbalization – the technique of *free association*.

Psychoanalysis recognizes the repression of affects as well as that of ideas and conceptions. Tensions that seek to make themselves known as sensations, feelings, and emotions may be held in check by opposing forces in the ego. Consequently, derivatives of repressed affects may appear as *substitute formations* – dreams, symptoms, or reaction formations.

In psychoanalytic theory, the ego may ward off unwanted perceptions by other means as well: negative hallucinations (filtering out some part of the external world); forgetting or misinterpreting outer events to achieve wish fulfillment; denial, etc. In every case, the defense operation represents the ego's activity of regulating id responses to perceptions of internal and external realities. In Fenichel's words:

> There are defensive attitudes against painful perceptions just as there are defenses against any pain. Nevertheless, in psycho-neuroses based on the blocking of discharge, the defenses against instinctual impulses remain in the foreground; defenses against perceptions (and affects) seem to be performed first and foremost in the service of defenses against instincts. Again: the neurotic conflict takes place between the ego and the id.
>
> Fenichel (1945: 131)

As Fenichel indicates, psychoanalytic tradition attributes distortions and omissions in reality perception to the ego's defenses against id drives. Analytical psychology, in contrast, inherits Jung's focus upon the influence of archetypes and complexes in broadening or narrowing the perceptual field.

Since Jung considered himself an empiricist rather than a theorist, his views on these processes must be extracted from his discussion of cases. He presents one outstanding case of knowing-and-not-knowing during his Tavistock Lectures (Jung 1935: 52–65) and in *Memories Dreams and Reflections* (Jung 1961: 115–17). He encountered the case during his early years at the Bergholzli, where he had discovered the "feeling-toned-complex" in the course of his diagnostic association studies. The subject was a married woman, the mother of two children. She had been admitted to the hospital under a diagnosis of schizophrenia. Suspecting a misdiagnosis, Jung inquired further into the case; he examined her dreams and subjected her to the association test. From the association test he discovered "that she was a murderess and I had learned many of the details of her secret."

The disturbance that led to this patient's hospitalization was believed to originate with the death of her favorite child, a daughter, from typhoid fever. But the association test revealed the true cause of her illness: she had allowed her children to drink the contaminated water that caused her daughter's typhus infection. Jung explains that he obtained from the test "information directly from the unconscious, and this information revealed a dark and tragic story." The woman had performed this reckless act during an epidemic. Water systems were known to be contaminated, but she had nonetheless permitted her daughter to sip river water from a bathing sponge; on the same occasion she had given her son a glass of the water to drink. At the time of hospitalization, the fact of her administration of the water to the children and its role in the death of her daughter was only dimly known to her. Her psychotic depression originated in this disparity between fact and comprehension. Depression, in this case, encapsulated a borderland of knowing.

Had Jung's patient administered the contaminated water to her children out of conscious intention, her depression would signify overwhelming feelings of guilt or, alternatively, an ego defense against recollection of her misdeed by means of repression. The features of the case, however, suggest something more complex. According to Jung's narrative, this fateful act was performed, not by conscious intention, but by *unconscious intention*. At the time of her daughter's infection the woman was living under the weight of an "incipient depression." Her depressive feelings originated with a devastating revelation: she learned from a friend that a man whom she once loved but had no hopes of winning did in truth love her and had been disappointed when she married another. Under the shadow of the "incipient depression," as Jung calls it, she administered the water to the children "unconsciously, or only half consciously."

The "unconscious intentionality" implicit in the case may be surmised from the disappointment which elicited her depression. Mourning a lost love and regretting her marriage, her children must have represented an obstacle to her happiness, a mistake. No loving mother would willfully infect her children with a deadly disease. However, unconscious complexes – with the drives and impulses that inhabit them – have aims of their own. If denied assimilation into consciousness, the shadow gains strength and, under certain circumstances, can subject the ego to its power.

In his lecture, published under the title "A Review of the Complex Theory," Jung states: "Where the realm of complexes begins the freedom of the ego comes to an end, for complexes are psychic agencies whose deepest nature is still unfathomed" (Jung 1948c: 104). The power Jung attributes to the complexes in their effect upon ego-consciousness was so great, it seems, that he showed little inclination to elaborate upon the ego's mechanisms of organization and defense. Instead, Jung was interested in the alterations of consciousness, which he attributed to the encroachment of a complex upon the ego. When writing of the ego, Jung emphasizes the *imposition* of affect upon ego-consciousness by the proximity of complexes to, or the assimilation of complexes into, ego-consciousness.

Every emotional state produces an alteration of consciousness which Janet called *abaissement du niveau mental*; that is to say there is a certain narrowing of consciousness and a corresponding strengthening of the unconscious. . . . The tone of the unconscious is heightened, thereby creating a gradient for the unconscious to flow towards the conscious. The conscious then comes under the influence of unconscious instinctual impulses and contents.

(Jung 1952: 446)

The murderous deed of Jung's patient, it seems, transpired under an *autohypnotic* state of consciousness. It signifies a dissociative act, induced by depression. According to Jung, she acted under a lowered threshold of consciousness, a state of mind described by Janet as an *abaissement du niveau mental*. The notion of the *abaissement* was pivotal for Jung, and it became a central concept in his theory of the nature and dynamics of the psyche.

Jung speaks of the *abaissement du niveau mental* in a variety of contexts, but most often when describing more extreme alterations of consciousness, such as seen in situations of mass hysteria or in serious psychopathologies. He appears to assume a gradient in intensity of the *abaissement* in different circumstances. Complexes, as organizers of emotions, can produce an *abaissement*, for their chief characteristic is affect. Since archetypes also express themselves as affects, ego-consciousness will be altered when in close proximity to an archetypal field. As formal factors responsible for the organization of unconscious psychic processes:

[Archetypes] have a "specific charge" and develop numinous effects that express themselves as *affects*. The affect produces a partial *abaissement du niveau mental*, for although it raises a particular content to a supernormal degree of luminosity, it does so by withdrawing so much energy from other possible contents of consciousness that they become darkened and eventually unconscious. Owing to the restriction of consciousness produced . . . there is a corresponding lowering of orientation which in its turn gives the unconscious a favorable opportunity to slip into the space vacated.

(Jung 1952: 436)

The theory of complex and archetype, therefore, is of profound significance to issues of conscience, will, intentionality of thought and deed – that is, to the question of human responsibility. Applying the energic model to the case of Jung's "murderess," we would assume her depression caused a lowering of conscious orientation and subjected her to "possession" by an unconscious complex. Given her circumstances, the possessing complex might be said to originate in the shadow – that unsavory area of the personal unconscious that harbors our most forbidden qualities. An *abaissement* may cause us to act out potentialities for which our conscious identity, shaped by adaptation to personal and collective moral standards, cannot account.

Jung's narrative further demonstrates his view of the psyche as containing fluid, rather than static, systems. It appears that the woman's "murder" of her child was unknown to her only in a relative sense. Jung's patient was able to take responsibility for the act once a subsequent experience activated synthetic functioning in the psyche, bridging the known-and-not-known content to consciousness. By confronting her with his suspicions, Jung awakened his patient to the painful truth of her role in her child's death, effecting a cure from her psychotic depression. Indeed, knowledge of her dissociative act resided just below the threshold of consciousness. In such a case knowing rests in a "twilight" zone, and can be accessed in consciousness only through the construction of associative links.

It is important to note that this particular case features two co-existing states of knowing-and-not-knowing. The case demonstrates how there can be *acts* that are known-and-not-known (many automatisms are common to daily life; they displace our keys or drive our cars); and there can be *truths* that are seen-and-not-seen. Both forms of knowing-and-not-knowing concern the intersection between internal, intrapsychic conditions and the external world.

As this case narrative demonstrates, Jung approached psychical problems from the point of view of the *unconscious* rather than from the perspective of the ego's operations of defense against such forces. In turning his inquiry away from ego operations and toward the contents of the unconscious, Jung laid ground for the development of a psychology that diverged from the tradition of Freud. This shift originated in his discovery of the feeling-toned-complex during the diagnostic association experiments. Complexes could be tracked with the appearance of memory blocks, compulsive repetitions of reaction, and assimilation of subsequent responses to the feeling tone of previously activated associations.

One of the most outstanding properties discovered was the complex's capacity to assimilate to itself new experiences consonant with its feeling tone. An unconscious complex may assimilate perceptions concurrent with its activation; both affect and the data of experience may subsequently recede with the complex back into the unconscious. These autonomous effects evince the degree to which complexes may constrict awareness of self and world. Observing the complex's capacity to assimilate experience into itself, Jung attributed distortions of perception and dissociations to the operations of the complex, rather than to the ego.

Jung began to speak of the complexes as "splinter psyches" – unconscious constellations comprised of affective life organized around core motifs. In the most dramatic example, a complex may act as a part-personality, as in multiple personality phenomena. Highly unconscious to the ego and therefore dramatically autonomous, such a complex may take control of the whole person leaving him, afterwards, with no memory of the event. In such cases of severe dissociation, all the experiences occurring while the ego was possessed by that particular complex retreat back into the unconscious with the complex. This extreme example demonstrates the significance of the complex generally for the functions of memory and the apperception of experience.

One might view the concept of the feeling-toned-complex as an alternative way of describing the process of repression. Experiences, thoughts, and percepts which are incompatible with the habitual attitude or convictions of the subject's conscious mind form psychic representations which, with other unconscious contents of a similar feeling tone, cluster around a nucleus and reside in the unconscious. To this point the concept of the complex harmonizes with the psychoanalytic portrait of repression. However, complex theory does not share the classical psychoanalytic attribution of the repressive function solely to ego operations. As we have seen, complex theory attributes memory loss, mental blockages, and myriad neurotic symptoms, first and foremost, to the autonomous operations of the activated complex. Once a complex comes into contact with the ego-complex, its influence will be determined by ego strength or weakness in relation to the complex's energic charge.

Most importantly, complex theory accounts for psychical phenomena extending far beyond the repressive function. While repressed complexes originate with conscious experience and adaptation, Jung attributed the formation of unconscious complexes to internally or externally derived experience that was never perceived:

> In the one case, there is an originally conscious content that became subliminal because it was repressed on account of its incompatible nature: in the other case, the secondary subject consists essentially in a process that never entered into consciousness at all because no possibilities exist there of apperceiving it. That is to say, ego-consciousness cannot accept it for lack of understanding, and in consequence it remains for the most part subliminal, although, from the energy point of view, it is quite capable of becoming conscious. It owes its existence not to repression, but to subliminal processes that were never themselves conscious.
>
> (Jung 1954: 174–5)

Jung takes up the topic of the *unconscious* complex in his essay "On Psychic Energy." Here he postulates the spontaneous formulation of complexes out of contents derived from the unconscious itself:

> The repression theory ... does not take into account those other cases in which a content of high energic intensity is formed out of unconscious material that is not in itself capable of becoming conscious, and so cannot be made conscious at all, or only with the greatest difficulty.
>
> (Jung 1948b: 11n19)

As in certain cases of dissociation, Jung accounts for the exclusion of such complexes from consciousness by suggesting that their contents are new and therefore cannot be accessed by established lines of communication between conscious and unconscious contents. He notes, "there are no existing associations and connecting bridges to the conscious contents. All these connections must first be laid down with considerable effort, for without them no consciousness is possible" (Jung 1948b: 11–12n19).

Often when speaking of knowing-and-not-knowing phenomena, we speak of truths that may become known under the right conditions. Jung, referring to the connecting bridge, points to the transformative work of reflection in illumining what was once elusive.

The metaphor of the bridge has become especially useful in my work as an analyst. Witnessing the construction of associative bridges over the course of years, I have come to see the ego's role as far from passive. For while unconscious processes are the primary focus of an analysis, the bridge to awareness can only be constructed by shifting between ego-consciousness and pre-conscious points of orientation within the psyche-soma.

Thus the complex process by which we contextualize external and internal experience presupposes the presence of an integral, observing ego. Despite Jung's emphasis upon the function of the archetypes in perception, ego defenses are clearly evident in the perceptual process. Through case examples we will thus explore the interplay of complex, archetype and ego in perception and consider identity and ego-strength as determinants in the repression, omission, or imagining of experience.

In so doing we reach beyond Jung's formulation by observing within the analytic process the ego's involvement in the inhibition of perceptions as well as its contribution to the organization of unconscious fragments of experience into coherent complexes. Michael Fordham's theory of ego development and object relations perspectives will illumine the ego's role in particular cases.

In as much as the ego, its functions, and its strengths and weaknesses are relevant to our topic, so too is the body, the focal point of self-awareness, involved in the transformation of the known-and-not-known into thought. In my view, somatic phenomena reflect two aspects of the perceptual process. As in several cases included in this study, psychosomatic illness may indicate a regression to infantile stages of perceptual functioning, and here a developmental perspective is necessary. But we also locate, apart from other psychoanalytic and Jungian authors, the body's role as a container for undigested fragments of experience, or, one might say, as a locus of the pre-conscious system. Here, the body takes on a prospective function in *cultivating* the formulation of feeling-toned-complexes and mental representations through sensation, injury, or illness. Turning to our first case study, we will see how injury and somatic imagery help one man gain ego-strength in relation to a possessing complex.

# Chapter 2

# Archetypal constrictions of identity

## A case of resolution through injury

As inherited modes of functioning, archetypes organize a broad range of operations in both animals and humans. This range begins with the automatic instinctual configurations that form behaviors and extends to the complex means by which ideas are produced and apprehended in human consciousness. Behavior and imagination are, of course, intricately connected; both are archetypally conditioned. This interplay between instinctive behavior patterns and our perceptual functioning will be examined by means of a case example.

When we speak of the archetype of the hero we generally refer to a mythologem that portrays ego-consciousness as a socio-historical as well as individual process in development. The archetype of the hero imposes upon us certain ideas and behaviors consonant with its mode of organization. This archetype embraces a sweeping range of experience; we are collectively and individually engaged in the hero's journey so long as our consciousness of self and world is expanding.

As with the individual, a collective's apprehension of archetypal configurations of meaning will be conditioned by characteristics unique to its history. These culturally conditioned characteristics reside within the collective consciousness, while the universal, constructive force of the archetype will always remain outside the reach of our awareness. In the West, the *archetype* of the hero continues to move us individually and collectively in many hidden ways. In the individual, it plays a star role in the unconscious organization of identity. But the myth of the hero is especially alive in the consciousness of boys and men.

Our first case of knowing-and-not-knowing concerns an analysand who was identified with a hero complex. This identification stemmed from the interplay of conscious and unconscious elements in his identity. The hero complex, which was in part known to him, encompassed personal and archetypal representations in tension with one another. This tension had been a motive force in his youth and had advanced his development in a positive direction. However, the complex's dynamic effect gave way to disruption as mid-life approached. While the *archetype* at the core of the complex still moved him to acquire new life experiences, his partly unconscious personal identification with the hero *image* constricted his apprehension of the world around him and impeded his psychological growth. His story demonstrates expansive and constrictive aspects of archetypal arrangement in thought, affect, and behavior.

Joseph presented himself for analysis with the complaint that he was having difficulty adapting to a new work environment. He summarized his situation as follows: he was an accomplished engineer who had been much valued by his former company. There his creativity and technical skill had won him a reputation as a gifted innovator. After ten years of playing a star role in the company, he had been ready for a new challenge; so when a larger, more prestigious corporation offered him a position, he happily accepted. He had recently taken up his new post and was applying the same revolutionary approach that had won him much success and recognition in his previous job. But he was disappointed to find that the corporate hierarchy repeatedly criticized or rejected his work. He desperately wanted to understand the problem, but the situation was beyond his comprehension. All he could figure was that his superiors must be misdirecting him and giving him mixed messages. He attributed the problem largely to conflict between members of the corporate hierarchy and to office politics.

While company politics certainly played a role in Joseph's difficulties, it was soon evident that the conflicts Joseph suffered at work stemmed from discordance between his revolutionary spirit and the traditional standards of his superiors – standards in concert with a conservative corporate culture. I was puzzled to find that Joseph could not fathom, much less respond to, the culture of this new working environment. In fact, the more he was exposed to evidence or statements of that kind, the more his revolutionary spirit drove him to greater and greater feats of innovation, which increasingly led to rejection. In the meantime, each failure dealt a blow to his self-esteem and neurotic symptoms formed incrementally – first anxiety, then panic attacks, and finally depression.

While working on this problem, it became clear to Joseph and me that his conscious identity was inextricably bound up with his professional persona as an innovative leader, someone who would impact his agency through the implementation of humanistic principles and far-reaching ideals. After some time, Joseph was able to admit that this mode of operating fell outside of corporate intentions. He was able to conceptualize his situation and showed some understanding of the factors of his personality that contributed to his failure. But out of a compulsion to prove himself, he stayed on his old course and continued to misconstrue project requirements; at times he intentionally defied his superiors' directives. Joseph was seeing-and-not-seeing his situation.

Trapped in a vortex of misperception and compulsion, Joseph dreamed of numinous figures whose appearance disclosed the mythologem encapsulating his identity. The following dream came to him at a particularly difficult juncture:

> I was in a country setting and there were employees of a company playing games, maybe on a company retreat. Two managers and I were observing the activities. The managers were talking about promoting a "perfect employee." The perfect employee was moving on horseback and hadn't yet crossed a small body of water. It wasn't a lake or a river, but was more like a shallow flood plain. Suddenly he started his horse galloping across the water and shot an arrow high in the air and it sailed and hit a bull's-eye far in the distance. It was an absolutely impossible shot. Everyone was amazed.
>
> Later in the dream I was alone with this man. We were looking at his bicycle, which he was repairing. We bet on something and I won a dollar from him. His bike didn't work because a chain, which was needed to connect two parts, was missing. I had an idea that I could fold the dollar and connect the two parts with it. The perfect employee got mad and said "no." I persevered and tried it. It was going to work, but this made him angry. He forced me to the ground, laid down on me and said "NO!" I said, "I won the dollar and you said I could do with it what I want to do with it, and I want to fix your bike." I backed off, realizing that this perfect employee wasn't emotionally perfect.

The dream disclosed Joseph's unconscious perception of his work environment as a mythological landscape. Joseph associated the perfect employee to the chivalrous knight, a hero on horseback. The figure of the hero, merged with Joseph's impossible expectations for himself as an employee, well portrayed the psychic conflict behind his symptoms. His unconscious expectations were utterly archetypal: he would ride into his new job like a hero on horseback and save the corporation by superhuman feats of innovation. This explained the compulsive aspect of his behavior.

We could also understand the hero complex as the factor behind Joseph's misapprehension of the corporate culture that surrounded him. His perceptual field was colored and narrowed by the possessing complex. So long as the hero complex dominated the perceptual system, the ego's synthetic operations could work only with those representations conforming to the heroic paradigm. Those elements of environment and personality incompatible with the archetypal structure were lost to him – not repressed but rather passed over. As yet Joseph possessed no associative bridge to link disparate components in his environment with consonant aspects of his personality.

Still, the dream-ego was on its way to discovering the problem of the hero-shadow, for he made contact with the hero and tried to assist him by fixing the severed bicycle. This image condenses myriad external and internal factors at play in the complex, and it has all the markings of a symbol. Among other things, the bicycle images a break in the harmony of elements belonging to the complex, elements which had at one time worked together in a dynamic and positive way. Our dream work revealed how, as a youth, Joseph modeled himself after heroes of song and myth. He had emulated the attitude and behavior of these figures and this helped him to overcome feelings of inferiority.

We now understood that the complex juxtaposed Joseph's inferiority feelings against representations of his many heroic victories. These oppositions circled around the hero image. The relative harmony of opposing elements in the complex proved tenuous. The change of work environment exposed the ego-complex once again to the inferior child image. The child in Joseph knew only one way to redress the imbalance: he was compelled to attain another heroic victory. This is the shadow aspect that attacks Joseph when he tries to fix the bicycle. Fortunately, the dream-ego gains insight into the problem when he acknowledges that "the perfect employee [isn't] emotionally perfect."

The dream further suggested that the analytic process of reflection had succeeded in linking consciousness with a small but significant quantum of energy from the complex – the dream ego had, after all, won a dollar from the hero and he was using this quantum as a tool to repair what was broken. The dream also showed that the energy available to ego-consciousness was not yet sufficient for overcoming the hero's assault on its efforts. Joseph was still highly invested in the heroic self-image, and his resistance to transformation would be formidable.

The image of the bicycle further pointed to the many positive and authentic qualities in Joseph's personality; he was a delightfully playful, sportive, bright and energetic man. But the complex was blocking his access to many of these qualities, qualities which could help him rise to his new situation.

Because Joseph was deeply moved by the insight which closed the dream, "that this perfect employee wasn't emotionally perfect," it seemed that the bridge to seeing the true nature of his work situation – as well as finding his own true nature – lay in the resolution of the childhood conflicts which had attached themselves to the hero complex. I attempted to lead our work in this direction; but like the hero of his dream, Joseph repeatedly sabotaged my efforts.

For months Joseph openly resisted reductive work. His stated aim in analysis was to find a rational solution to a current problem. We thus concentrated our efforts on analysis of dynamics at work and related dream imagery. Nonetheless, Joseph occasionally allowed me to relate his heroic deeds and attitudes back to those few episodes of his childhood story he had shared with me. These occasions slowly edged Joseph toward affective contact with the personal components in the complex. In addition, Joseph's dreams helped us work toward the construction of an associative bridge to the archetypal image through amplification of the hero's journey – the only means, according to Jung, by which we can perceive the effects of the archetype on the personality. The real transformation of Joseph's conscious attitude, however, came after his body entered the dialogue by means of a sporting accident.

About six months after Joseph dreamed of the "perfect employee", his relations at work were dramatically disintegrating and his depression had reached an alarming depth. To give himself some relief from the pressures at work, he took his family off for a ski-holiday. A few days after his departure he called from the hospital to tell me that he had fallen and damaged his knee which now had to be surgically repaired.

When Joseph returned to analysis, we talked extensively of the incidents leading up to his accident. I could see that the circumstances of his accident replicated the dynamics which were causing him difficulties at work. He had not skied for many years. Although he had previously acquired no more than a beginner's skill, he proudly mastered the beginners' slopes on his first day out. Making further progress on his second day, he felt elated. He then made the fateful decision to tackle the slope for advanced skiers. Reaching far beyond his known capacity, he made a hard fall, ending the family's vacation and badly damaging his knee. In addition to the bodily injury he now suffered, he had incurred the wrath of his wife and this obligated him to reflect upon his actions.

Seeing the figure of the hero behind his recklessness, I reminded Joseph of the dream of the "perfect-employee" and related the hero's behavior to his compulsion to make the "impossible shot" while skiing. In the months that it took for Joseph's knee to mend, we returned many times to the ski incident and its relation to the hero of his dream. Together we entered a dialogue with this hero in the shadow. The dialogue continued over the course of two years in which time the energy formerly bound up with the complex was released by small increments into consciousness. His depressive symptoms lifted concurrent with a strengthening of his capacity to take in messages from his environment, synthesize their meaning, and adapt accordingly.

Clearly our dialogue with the hero-complex was bearing fruit, but much of Joseph's personal history and affective life remained outside of the reflective process. He was developing a more objective attitude toward his work environment but he kept his distance from the childhood inferiority feelings still active in him. He was responding responsibly to his employers' directives but his efforts taxed and fatigued him. Despite the long hours he dedicated to his assignments, his performance was at best mediocre.

He assessed his situation and decided to make a fresh start with another company. As he was settling into this new post he was once again motivated to break new ground for the agency. As we sat together one day, Joseph spoke animatedly to me of his plans, and I feared he might revert to the old heroic pattern. But I said nothing.

Then Joseph remembered a dream. The imagery centered upon a hero figure from his youth and the knee injured in the accident of the previous winter:

> I was standing before Sam who was sitting with his head facing my legs. I'd peeled away skin on my knee exposing what looked like meat on a chicken's leg. Innards from my knee lay on the floor, and black worms moved among the flesh. I wanted Sam to eat the meat from my knee but he was reluctant to do so. I encouraged him and he took a taste. He said that it tasted good, was a bit sweet, but it was too disgusting so he didn't want anymore.

This dream set the ground for important changes in Joseph's identity through the integration of the hero problem. As Joseph told his dream, the atmosphere between us took on an uncanny, numinous quality. I was impressed by the ritual imagery of the dream, and by the juxtaposition of *numinosum* and feelings of disgust transmitted in the telling of it.

According to Joseph his dream-ego empathically shared in Sam's repulsion when consuming the putrified flesh of the knee. This led Joseph to speak at length about Sam as a man who, like himself, was motivated by strong aspirations and ideals. Sam was a man of outstanding academic accomplishment. He dedicated his life to assisting trauma victims in an impoverished inner-city neighborhood. He further challenged social conventions by raising his family in a fairly dangerous area of the city. On the whole, Sam represented a rather romantic figure for Joseph. Joseph especially admired Sam for his adventurous spirit, which had taken him a few years back to the Near East where he crossed a desert on camelback in the company of a Bedouin tribe.

Sam, Joseph said, is someone who lives his ideals. But as he said this, Joseph recalled how he hadn't heard from Sam for two years. This lapse in communication represented a departure from Sam's usual habit of contacting Joseph at each New Year. In fact, Joseph had a premonition that something had changed in Sam's life. He had the fantasy that Sam's marriage had ended, or that he had moved on to a more conventional job.

My thoughts turned to the role Joseph's heroic ideals had played in the shaping of his identity and to the imprint this had made on

his professional life. It seemed that the dream issued a warning
against a reversion to the old attitude. The dream ego, erotically
invested in the hero-ideal represented by Sam, pursues a ritual
*conjunctio*. Surprisingly – and the element of surprise signifies an
important moment – both figures in the dream experience an
instinctive reaction against the ritual. The worms apprise them to
the fact that the flesh from the gaping knee is putrefied. The images
presented – flesh and worms – are perceived and contextualized.
The instinct to survive enters the perceptive field and the ritual is
interrupted. In this regard, Joseph's fantasies about changes in
Sam's life seemed profoundly significant. Further associations followed, and then a sudden insight: Joseph realized that the knee on
which Sam feeds in the dream is the same knee that had been
injured in the skiing accident.

A rapid succession of associations followed, evincing the power of
such an image for bridging the gap that separates ego-consciousness from the overshadowing complex. Joseph saw the connection
between the "overaggressive idealism" behind his ski accident and
his current compulsion to perform heroic feats in his new job. He
was then flooded by childhood memories bearing similar themes.
The image of the injured knee – and the hero's repulsion to what
it signified – was the determinative link in the associative chain that
we had long been constructing. The hero complex, once far removed
from consciousness, could now be apprehended in consciousness.
No longer diffusely aware, but rather with an unprecedented clar-
ity, Joseph was cognizant of his life pattern: "I see now that my
ideals are too grand. I trip over myself when trying to implement
them, because there are too many obstacles. Then my creative
energy withdraws and I feel insecure."

After this time Joseph used his analysis to strengthen his identity
and broaden his professional persona. He adopted a more prag-
matic attitude at work and, at the same time, found appropriate
outlets for his authentically innovative spirit.

I believe that the strongest force in the transformation of Joseph's
personality was the injury he incurred during his ski holiday.
At this time, he had gained some measure of insight into attitudes
and behaviors that put him at odds with his superiors and impeded
his apprehension of the corporate culture. But he had also avoided
all contact with the more difficult affective components residing
in the possessing complex. His resistance engendered the depression
he hoped to escape by means of a holiday. Repression plays a

significant role in Joseph's psychological journey, but a distinction must be made between the effects of repression on Joseph's apprehension of his *internal life* and *its effects on his perceptions of the outer world*. The perceptual oversight that falsified his vision of the surrounding culture originated with the *archetypal functioning* of the complex, a component that by definition is unknowable. The repressive function contributed to the *coloring* of his perceptions, no doubt, but it is important to distinguish between the elements of the complex which belonged to the personal unconscious as repressions, and the perceptual structures imposed by the complex's organizing archetype.

We might also note that at the time of the injury, Joseph's heroic behavior had become compulsive. This signified the growing distance between opposing images in the complex: on one side, inferiority feelings from childhood; and on the other, the triumphant hero image. Since the ego was not yet prepared to integrate the difficult affects contained in the disturbing complex, the Self utilized the body as a means of bypassing his resistance to knowing.

It is as though Joseph, through injury, reenacted some unknown early wounding of his spirit. Yet at the same time, it was the *hero* whose knee was injured, not the child's. The hero pushed him beyond his capacity, and the resulting injury served to bring him closer to the source of his conflict. Event and injury syncretically spanned the oppositions behind Joseph's suffering. The injury spans (1) the divide between conscious and unconscious positions (the heroic component of ego-consciousness opposed to the hidden wounded child); and (2) the opposition between images of hero and the weak and inferior youth contained in the complex. By means of the transcendent function, the injured knee is offered as the third option; this new symbol opened the door for more insight and, eventually, resolution of the complex.

The symbolic work of Joseph's injury bore fruit in several stages. Most importantly, we were able to draw meaningful connections between his life pattern and the archetype of the hero through amplification. This helped us to perceive the injurious aspects of Joseph's revolutionary attitude. Second, recent injuries to Joseph's self-esteem could be linked to the inferiority feelings he suffered in childhood, and he came to understand the compensatory function of the hero pattern. Then finally, his dream-presentation of the injured knee to a hero figure opened his consciousness to the truth of his own true nature: he was not wholly a hero, nor a wounded child, but rather someone with unique gifts and a full range of personal qualities and emotions.

# Chapter 3

# Albert Speer's twilight of evil

## A case of near-death awakening

Each day in a life contains some word, gesture or act which sub-sequent reflection judges unworthy or regrettable. Mercifully, con-science allows us to live in relative peace with such daily indications of our flawed humanity. But each life also harbors deeds, decisions, or allegiances of grave consequence, and such things haunt us in their irrevocability. Such is the Third Reich's legacy to the collective conscience of the West; it signifies that moment in history which will forever testify to the collective force of the individual capacity for evil.

Much has been said of the political, social, and economic factors which created and sustained Hitler's reign of madness. If such a moment in modern history attests to our human susceptibility to possession en masse by powerful archetypal forces of destruction, individual cases of dissent remind us that conscience is a personal rather than collective attribute. Still, we have the most to learn, not from those few heroic individuals who stood against the tide of mass hysteria under National Socialism, but from those who were swept up by the collective force of the movement. We may glean from the post-war reflections of certain affected individuals crucial insight into the operations of the collective psyche: those factors prefiguring mass movements; the dissociative operations of the mass-mind; as well as the psychic-somatic factors counterposing its dominance over the individual. The memoirs of Albert Speer, Hitler's architect and Minister of Armaments during the war, are particularly instructive in this regard.

This chapter reviews the tension between mass-mindedness and personal conscience in the life of Albert Speer. We will examine the circumstances behind his conversion to National Socialism, his rela-tionship with Hitler, and the means by which he blinded himself to

Hitler's evil. Of the 18 men who were convicted of crimes against humanity by the Nuremberg court, Speer was one of only seven men who escaped the death penalty. In the final judgment, it could not be proven that Speer had known of the regime's program of genocide against European Jews, despite the fact that he had once been Hitler's closest associate and, for a short time, had been poised to succeed the Führer. If Speer, as he claimed, had no knowledge of the extermination program until the time of the Nuremberg trials, his case demonstrates how the perceptual field can be narrowed indefinitely, even under non-traumatic conditions. (I hold that while Speer, as Minister of Armaments and Munitions, inflicted trauma upon the victims of war, the stress of his administrative responsibility had by no means imposed acute psychic trauma upon him personally.)

The issue at the center of Speer's post-war life – from the beginning of his 20 years imprisonment until his death in September 1981 – was Hitler's murder of the Jews. As the journalist Gitta Sereny puts it: "While he sincerely grasped every opportunity to reiterate his sorrow and his pain at having been . . . 'a part of a government that committed such crimes', he was totally incapable of saying that he had known about them at the time" (Sereny 1995: 340). Speer, like countless others who did not share his proximity to the Führer, lived in a twilight state of knowing, a state that 40 years of self-examination could not fully penetrate.

Our discussion of the case will be based upon Gitta Sereny's extensive interviews with Speer, documented in her meticulous study entitled *Albert Speer: His Battle with Truth* (1995). Sereny, a London-based journalist of Hungarian origin, has dedicated much of her life to the study of "moral impotence" in Hitler's Germany. Her study documents the gradual process by which Speer, who was in many ways a man of excellence, allowed himself to become an agent of Hitler's evil.

## Outlines of Speer's career

Albert Speer first came into personal contact with Hitler in 1933 while he was commissioned small architectural jobs for the National Socialist party in Berlin. Hitler soon displayed a personal interest in him, an interest due partly to the fact that Speer proved he could build in record time, and largely to Speer's striking upper class demeanor: he was handsome, modest and restrained, and possessed an air of quiet competence. A relationship – undoubtedly homoerotic in tone – quickly developed between them. Hitler was known to become inspirited in Speer's presence, and he soon included Speer in the daily mealtime gatherings of his inner circle. A large quota of the party's construction projects fell into Speer's hands, and the two enjoyed many private hours talking animatedly of their shared interest in architecture. Their association was the closest either man had come to deep friendship.

Soon Speer was considered Hitler's favorite, but he liked to think of himself as an independent contractor rather than a government man. When in 1937 Speer was appointed as *Generalbauinspektor* (GBI) for the construction of Berlin, he accepted on the condition that he assume the post as a private architect. Thus when the Nuremberg court reviewed his dossier, Speer insisted that he had worked for Hitler as a private citizen and had not served as a Reich officer until his appointment as Minister in 1942. This was technically true. However, the record shows that Hitler had been grooming Speer for higher office since the time of his appointment as GBI.

As Chief Inspector for the reconstruction of Berlin, Speer headed a staff of 85. Associates and employees from those years confirm Speer's claim that he was "unpolitical," despite the fact that he stood in Hitler's inner circle. He gave employment to individuals on the basis of their competence, not their political standing, and this included numerous individuals of Jewish descent. The efficiency and productivity of his offices won Speer his reputation as a managerial genius with special skills in delegation.

As Chief Inspector, Speer joined the ranks of those whose minds were converted to Hitler's vision for Germany. Many of the ideas for the reconstruction of Berlin originated with Hitler. Indeed, it was Speer's capacity to respond to Hitler's vision, to expand and develop Hitler's ideas, which accounts for his rapid rise to power. This, coupled with Speer's proven organizational genius, led to Speer's appointment as Minister for Armaments at the inception of the war.

His move in 1942 from favored architect to Reich official represented a radical shift in duties, but such a shift is not incomprehensible given the atmosphere of Hitler's "court" in the intervening years. Speer had not only demonstrated managerial brilliance, but had coordinated an enormous network of supply production and shipment for Hitler's mammoth construction works. The most compelling factor behind Speer's appointment, however, was his emotional bond with Hitler. The mutual admiration between the two men, each incapable of expressing personal feeling, accounts for Speer's enormous productivity. In the end, Speer's determination to please Hitler prolonged the operation of Germany's war machine beyond all reasonable expectation.

## Hitler's seduction of Speer: mass mind or basic fault?

When *Mishmar* correspondent Eugen Kolb asked Carl Jung whether or not the executioners of Hitler's plans were equally "psychopathic" to Hitler, Jung's answer was affirmative. Hitler, Jung responded, "was able to work on all those who compensated their inferiority complex with social aspirations and secret dreams of power. As a result he collected an army of social misfits, psychopaths, and criminals around him, to which he also belonged." Jung goes on to note that at the same time Hitler gripped the unconscious of normal people who are "always naive and fancy themselves utterly innocent and right" (Jung 1945: 605). While the former category adequately characterizes a great number of Hitler's henchmen, it does not fit the profile of Albert Speer as rendered by his associates and the outsiders who knew him. Nor can it be said that Speer fell into the category of the naive "normal" people. Unlike the majority of Third Reich officials, Speer came from the Protestant *haute bourgeoisie*, was politically as well as religiously uncommitted in his youth, and was described as unconventional by his university friends (Sereny 1995: 64–73). The son of a wealthy architect and a society matron, Speer, unlike his university colleagues, did not suffer the economic hardships that had afflicted the greatest majority of Germans after World War I.

The young Albert Speer had no interest in politics. While Hitler was captivating audiences and winning the enthusiasm of university students with his fiery speeches in the early 1920s, Speer remained practically oblivious to the political climate that surrounded him. His letters to girlfriend Margarete Weber, written from his Karlsruhe college in 1923 and then in 1924 from the Institute of Technology in Munich, speak mostly of walks taken, concerts and plays attended, his studies, and include only passing references to coal shortages or transport difficulties. Speer's distance from the political climate of his contemporaries is all the more notable if one compares his correspondence with the diary notes of Joseph Goebbels – also a university student at the time. In the following example, an entry from June 1924, Goebbels writes of the contest between the People's Freedom Party and the National Socialist Workers' Party:

> It's a confrontation of Munich and Berlin, or one can also say of Hitler and Ludendorff. There can be no doubt whom I will join: the young, who really seek to create a new human being.

The 4 July entry reads:

> We must stop spouting phrases and experimenting. We must seriously begin the work . . . and throw out the Jewish rabble who will not submit to the concept of a responsible people's community . . . As the earth cries for rain in the heat of the summer, so Germany longs for the One Man. God, bring about a miracle for the German people! . . . I am desperate for my fatherland. . . . Help me, God, I'm at the end of my strength. . . .
>
> (Sereny 1995: 67–8)

Goebbels' political zeal and emotionality was by no means exceptional in the early years of Hitler's arrival on the political scene. As Sereny notes:

> This was the feeling among young – and many older – Germans: Hitler was by no means a sudden phenomenon, arriving on the scene unannounced, unknown or, as has often been claimed, ridiculed. His picture, on the contrary, was on every front page for months and years, and his name on all lips.
>
> (Sereny 1995: 68)

Exceptionally, Speer distanced himself from the collective feelings of his contemporaries. He tells Sereny:

> Politics to me was noise and vulgarity. If I thought of it at all, it was only as an interruption to the quiet and the concentration I sought. My ideal, you see, was my teacher, who whispered; his concept of life and of art, which was pure and simple: fanaticism of any kind simply had no place in it.
>
> (Sereny 1995: 70)

The beloved teacher to whom he referred was Heinrich Tessenow, Speer's professor of architecture at the Berlin Institute of Technology from 1925 to 1927. Tessenow, who impressed Speer with his love of nature and simplicity, was a declared anti-Nazi; ironically, his course in Berlin became a center for Nazi agitation. The fact that Speer remained aloof to these currents may reflect the esteem he held for Tessenow as mentor and role model. His association with Tessenow continued after his graduation in 1927 when Tessenow employed Speer as his graduate assistant. During his interviews with Sereny, Speer had occasion to compare his relationship to Tessenow with the relationship he later developed with Hitler:

> I admired – no, I worshipped [Tessenow], but it never became a personal relationship in any way. He was much too closed up, really quite a bit like me. My feelings for him were very different from those I would later have for Hitler: Tessenow could give me nothing tangible – no "task", no goal in life, if you see what I mean. My admiration for him, therefore, was much more detached, much freer really, than eventually for Hitler; it was . . . purer.
>
> (Sereny 1995: 71–2)

As this comment reveals, Speer did not yet share his contemporaries' political passions, but he did harbor the seed of hero-worship so characteristic of young men of his era.

Of course, Speer's disregard for the social, economic, and political struggles of his countrymen reflects the privilege of his social class as well as his character. While a majority of his contemporaries had little chance of suitable employment, Speer's teaching appointment under Tessenow provided a moderate salary; but he also received a monthly stipend from his wealthy father. Financially stable and with a promising career before him, Speer married Margarete Weber in 1928. Meanwhile, Speer's students – all of whom had been won over to the National Socialist camp – pressed him to attend political rallies.

Speer lived and worked in the center of the storm; nonetheless he kept his distance from the movement for several years. Then, in late 1930, he succumbed to the pressure. More out of curiosity than conviction, Speer attended Hitler's December 1930 address to students in Berlin. Over 5000 were in attendance – professors as well as students. Speer describes the event in a letter to his daughter, written from Spandau prison:

What was decisive for me was a speech Hitler made to students, and which my students finally persuaded me to attend. From what I had read in the opposition press, I expected to find a screaming, gesticulating fanatic in uniform, instead of which we were confronted with a quiet man in a dark suit who addressed us in the measured tones of an academic. I am determined one day to look up newspapers of that time to see just what it was he said that so impressed me. But I don't think he attacked the Jews.

(Sereny 1995: 79)

Now over half a century later, the gesticulating, fanatical image of Hitler dominates our collective memory, and this leaves us in the vulnerable position of forgetting his genius. Hitler won a nation to his vision by means of his uncanny ability to intuit the sentiments of diverse audiences. He embodied the passions and indignation of the despairing working class, and played up to group responses; but he could also be reflective and restrained when addressing educated audiences.

Until this first personal encounter with Hitler, Speer had been immune to contagion from the mass. Now, however, he was unable to withstand the affective force of the crowd. His conversion to the movement began the moment Hitler approached the podium. As he recalls, Hitler appeared and was "greeted with incredible enthusiasm. Receptive as I am to atmosphere, already this had its effect on me: I felt goosepimples going down my spine" (Sereny 1995: 80). It was a fateful moment; Speer's thinking conformed immediately to the perceptual frame imposed by the archetype, as can be discerned by his first impression of Hitler:

Above all else . . . I felt he was a human being; I mean by that, I felt he cared: not only about Germany, which in his own terrible way of course he did, but that he cared about people. If you like, though it would never have occurred to me to put it like that at the time, that he cared about me . . . I mean . . . about us, the young, individually. I am still convinced now that this was his greatest gift: to convey, not in words but by a kind of mass – and individual – hypnosis, that he cared about each of us, even, if you forgive the term, that he loved us. I didn't expect to feel that, you see; I abhor, yes, I abhor vulgarity and loudness, and that's what I had associated with him before that night. So you see, I made a double mistake in judgement, one before that night – for certainly he was not vulgar – and one afterwards, for certainly, at least in the accepted sense of the word, he could not love. But it took me years – a kind of lifetime – to realize that.

(Sereny 1995: 82)

His conversion had little to do with Hitler's message, the content of which escaped his memory entirely. Rather, it was the personage of Hitler that decisively moved him.

To understand Speer's conversion to Hitler's movement and the self-deceptions that later blinded him to Hitler's criminality, both collective and personal factors must be considered. In numerous papers written during and after the Nazi period, Jung attributed the Hitler phenomenon to collective possession by the hero archetype and to the archaic spirit of Wotan. Above all he attributed the rise of mass movements in the age to the objective psyche's compensatory function. As early as 1919, Jung warned of the dangers of this process:

> If this animation [of the collective unconscious] is due to a complete breakdown of all conscious hopes and expectations, the danger arises that the unconscious may take the place of conscious reality. Such a state is morbid. We actually see something of this kind in the present Russian and German mentality. An outbreak of violent desires and impossible fantasies among the lower strata of the population is analogous to an outburst from the lower strata of the unconscious in an individual.
>
> (Jung 1946: 234)

In 1936, however, Jung attributed the compensation to the demise of Christianity and considered social, economic, and political ills as secondary causal factors. The "Mediterranean father-archetype of the just, order-loving, benevolent ruler" had been shattered, according to Jung, and Wotan, as the "nationalist God" had filled the vacuum. He believed the ecstatic nature of this archaic archetype gave the movement its peculiar character:

> Perhaps we may sum up this general phenomenon as *Ergriffenheit* – a state of being seized or possessed. The term postulates not only an *Ergriffener* (one who is seized) but also an *Ergreifer*

(one who seizes). Wotan is an *Ergreifer* of men, and, unless one wishes to deify Hitler – which has indeed actually happened – he is really the only explanation. . . . The impressive thing about the German phenomenon is that one man, who is obviously "possessed," has infected a whole nation to such an extent that everything is set in motion and has started rolling on its course towards perdition.

(Jung 1936: 184–5)

Those who worked closely with Hitler used similar language when describing the effects of the Führer's presence. For example, Goring once commented to Finance Minister Hjalmar Schacht, "every time I stand before the Führer, my heart drops into the seat of my pants" (Sereny 1995: 137). After the war Hitler's associates used the word "hypnotized" when describing his ability to bend people to his will. This experience of possession elicited accompanying feelings of pleasure; its quality is ecstatic, one might even say erotic. As Sereny notes, "even though many of those who had lived in his immediate surroundings professed to deplore Hitler's crimes, there was not only a defensive but, curiously enough, an almost pleasurable element in their descriptions of these hypnotic powers they had been subjected to" (Sereny 1995: 250). As Speer once said to Sereny:

I ask myself time and again how much of it was a kind of auto-suggestion. One thing is certain: everyone who worked closely with him for a long time was exceptionally dependent on him. However powerful they were in their own domain, close to him they became small and timid.

(Sereny 1995: 136–7)

Of course, the archetypal constellation around Hitler affected the feeling judgment of a nation, not just those who were close to him. As the individual accounts testify, contact with Hitler produced intensive affective states and consequent disturbances in cognitive functions – fundamental signs of archetype and complex activation as was demonstrated by Jung's association studies.

At the same time, not every person who came into contact with Hitler fell under his spell. The example of Speer's own father is instructive in this regard. Herr Albert Friedrich Speer, an "old-time liberal," sympathized with the Pan-European Movement which favored free-market economics, reduction in trade and movement barriers, and promoted the idea that a nation should be defined by its culture, not by its race. He stayed firm in his rejection of the National Socialist agenda, even after Speer's architectural appointments and later appointment as Minister. Nonetheless, Herr Speer was proud of his son when his work for Hitler won him public acclaim (Speer won the World Fair prize for Germany in 1937). Herr Speer met Hitler by chance one evening while attending the theatre with his son. Hitler, who was seated in his private box that evening, spied Speer with the older gentleman and sent his adjutant over to say that if the gentleman was Speer's father, he would like to meet him. In Speer's words:

> As soon as my father stood facing Hitler, I saw him pale and tremble – his whole body shuddered as if he had the ague. He didn't appear even to hear Hitler's hymn of praise about me; he just bowed without having said a word and left the box. Outside, he stood for a long moment breathing deeply, then the trembling stopped. Stupidly, I thought he was just unbearably moved, and I was surprised by his unusual display of feeling. Although we had never touched each other in my life except on formal occasions, I remember I touched or perhaps even tried to take his arm. He pulled away quite sharply. Now, of course, I understand: emotionally, politically and, yes, morally on a different plane from the Nazis, he had somehow felt that night that other "id" in Hitler – whatever it was – which I never sensed until years later.
>
> (Sereny 1995: 158)

We can assume that while Herr Speer's liberal sympathies may have predisposed him to dislike Hitler, the kind of response here described suggests he encountered something in Hitler for which he was unprepared. Without the veil of archetypal projection to cloud his instincts, Herr Speer sensed the evil Hitler embodied – something which Hitler's associates, even after all the atrocities were revealed, could not acknowledge.

As the record shows, an insignificant number of individuals perceived Hitler's true nature. It bears mentioning that in the early years of Hitler's rule, even outsiders – persons who stood well outside of the mass euphoria of National Socialism – praised Hitler as a leader of outstanding ability. During his first years as Chancellor, health, social security and old age benefits had been successfully expanded. Public works included a network of *Autobahnen*, traffic-free city centers, and the development of parks. Churchill once said that he hoped Great Britain would have a man like Hitler in times of peril; authors such as Gertrude Stein and George Bernard Shaw praised and defended him, to name just a few (Sereny 1995: 27).

Inside Germany, however, all was achieved by conscious as well as unconscious manipulations of the public. Allied with the collective projection onto Hitler was the steady process of indoctrination – first rallies and propaganda, followed by discriminatory laws, then the first pogrom against the Jewish community in modern German history (*Kristallnacht*) – which made violence by the state acceptable to young and old alike. With advances in employment, a stable currency, and a wave of optimism among the young, Hitler was soon able to appropriate Austria, Czechoslovakia, declare war on Poland, carry out his euthanasia program on Germans and Austrians, and build his extensive network of concentration and labor camps throughout his extended Reich – much of it with the cooperation of the rest of the Western world. The final outcome of this momentum in terms of mass conquest and unsurpassed murder is well known.

If Speer's conversion to National Socialism is mainly attributable to the collective archetypal constellation around the Führer, his incapacity to apperceive Hitler's criminality demands further explanation. Given his close working relationship with Hitler, Speer had ample opportunity to witness Hitler's megalomania or intuit his darkest intentions, even if unspoken. It can be shown retrospectively that Speer demonstrated an aptitude for knowing-and-not-knowing modes of consciousness from the earliest years of his association with Hitler. In his discussions with Sereny, Speer enumerated many occurrences that should have alerted him to Hitler's criminality and megalomania in the early years of their association – occurrences that he was able to contextualize and cognitively formulate only after his projections onto Hitler were withdrawn.

One early example concerns the 1934 "Rohm Putsch," the Nazi murder of four SA officers under Hitler's leadership, one of whom (Ernst Rohm, SA Chief of Staff) had been on a "Du" basis with Hitler. Speer explains: "You see, when it happened, just like when other things happened later – Austria, Czechoslovakia and so on – I suspect all I would have thought, if I thought at all, was that as Hitler was doing it, it had to be right" (Sereny 1995: 117).

For example, Speer recalls how in the spring of 1937 Hitler visited his architectural offices to view plans for the reconstruction of Berlin. Looking at the seven-foot-high model of the stadium, Speer pointed out to Hitler that the athletic field did not conform to the proportions prescribed by the Olympic Committee. Hitler responded, "That's immaterial. In 1940 the Games will be held in Tokyo, but after that, for all time to come, they will take place in Germany, in this stadium. And then it is we who will prescribe the necessary dimensions." Speer adds:

> Thinking of this later, it was almost incredible to me that this didn't open my eyes. I was after all a sportsman. . . . I knew perfectly well that the whole universal concept of the event presupposed a change of venue every four years. How could he have thought he could bend the powerful world of sports to his will? How could he have wanted it? How could I not have realized that day that he was mad? Well, I didn't; I can almost still see myself smiling in admiration at his prophetic words. He had drawn me into his madness.
>
> (Sereny 1995: 154)

Speer especially despaired of his ongoing lack of reaction to Hitler's words and measures against the Jews. Of *Kristallnacht* (9 November 1938) Speer only remembers that he was disturbed by the disorder in the streets: the broken windows and smoldering buildings.

In the post-war atmosphere many people, particularly former Nazis, claimed ignorance of such things, not only to others, but often to themselves. Knowledge of Nazi crimes in the emotional climate that followed the war seemed as great a threat as any acts they might have committed. Fear of blame extended to citizens of towns and villages. People whose windows virtually overlooked the roll-call squares of Germany's camps swore that they had never known they were concentration camps, even though some could see the punishments, beatings and executions being carried out almost daily. Speer, however, did not attribute his silence or his incomprehension of internal and external measures against the Jews to fear, but rather to his need to maintain his heroic image of Hitler: "I continued to wear blinkers, long after anyone who wanted to see the truth could see it, because they enabled me to hold on to the two things which had become my life: my power and my feelings for Hitler" (Sereny 1995: 162).

The depth of Speer's love and dependence upon Hitler, and the consequent intransigence of his projections onto the Führer, was undoubtedly linked with personal as well as collective factors. As we have seen, Speer had not suffered the same social and economic ills of his working-class associates. His background in no way predisposed him to be drawn to the National Socialist agenda. It rather appears that Speer's vulnerability before Hitler was largely due to his unresolved quest for paternal love and approval. The roots of Speer's projection onto Hitler as one who "cared about *me* . . . about us, the young, *individually* [my italics]" go back to Speer's adoration for a father who did not reciprocate his love. "What I felt for [father] was more than respect," he confessed to Sereny, "even more than love, I think. I revered him, but I honestly don't think he noticed I was there." By Speer's account, his father's love and affection extended exclusively to the youngest son, while his mother favored the eldest. His brothers took advantage of his isolation and tormented him mercilessly. Falling through the cracks of family affection, it was Speer's governess, a French Jew, who caught and held him emotionally: "the only warmth I ever felt at home was from our French governess, Mlle Blum" (Sereny 1995: 42).

As a young man, Speer formed the pattern of self-negation and paralysis before the demands of his father that he later reenacted in his relationship with Hitler. For instance, Speer wished to pursue a career in mathematics, for which he was especially gifted. His father vetoed his choice on the basis of its impracticality. Rather than risking conflict, Speer acceded and adopted his father's profession. This decision was fateful for Speer, not just because his practice as an architect placed him in Hitler's path, but also because he did not feel called to architecture. As a result, he constantly doubted his talent as an architect, and this imposed upon him an insatiable need to prove himself professionally.

The collective projection onto Hitler, as hero and father of the people, intersected with Speer's unresolved need for paternal love and approval. Hitler's favor bolstered Speer's confidence; so long as he had the Führer's approval, pervasive feelings of insecurity were alleviated. Yet, as with his attempts to please his father, that approval was won at the price of his independence and will. It was, I believe, the perpetuation of this constellation of the father complex in relation to Hitler that kept Speer in a perceptual twilight for more than a decade.

By the time of Speer's appointment as Minister of Armaments, the regime's program of genocide was well underway. At least 12 high-ranking German officers of the General staff and a greater number of top Nazi officials knew of the plans for eradication of European Jews as early as the spring of 1941. By the end of 1941, one million Soviet Jews and non-Jews, including civilians, had been shot. Gassing operations had begun in Chelmno and three other extermination camps in occupied Poland were completed by the spring of 1942. By December 1942 more than one million Jewish men, women and children had already been eliminated by gas, and the number of Soviet Jews shot by SS men and regular soldiers had reached almost two million.

Sereny believes that so long as Speer's relationship with Hitler had been based on their mutual passion for architecture, Hitler would have kept Speer "at arm's length from unsuitable or unpalatable matters. . . . includ[ing] his plans for murder." But with Speer's change of position to Minister of Armaments and his increasing involvement in the mobilization of labor for arms and munitions production, it seems incomprehensible that Speer would not be exposed to evidence pointing to the fuller reality of the regime's program of genocide: "in the world within which Speer now moved, directives were issued which, even if he didn't see them, in the final analysis, he had to know about, or sense their consequences" (Sereny 1995: 367).

One example given is Himmler's directive to five SS agencies regarding Jewish works, dated 2 October 1942. The directive orders all "so-called armament workers" occupied exclusively in tailor, fur and shoe workshops be put into concentration camps in Warsaw and Lublin. Point three of the directive states: "The Jewish workers will be replaced by Poles while a few large concentration camp workshops will for the moment carry on in the General Government camps. Eventually, however, in line with the Führer's instructions, these Jews too will disappear" (Sereny 1995: 367). Two months later Fritz Sauckel, who recruited forced labor for Speer's armaments ministry, implemented Himmler's directive. When Sereny questioned Speer on the developments during this period, he told her, "This is when I should have begun to realize what was happening. This was the point, I now think, when, had I *wanted* to, I could have detected hints." And when asked what he would have done if he had found out at that point, Speer answered with remorse, "I would somehow have gone on trying to help that man win his war" (Sereny 1995: 368).

We might assume with Speer that after the war erupted his former tendency toward perceptual oversight gave way to a more active process of self-deception. But the situation was complex. Objective factors colluded with archetypal arrangements in producing twilight states of awareness among all members of Hitler's government. Hitler was a master of compartmentalization. His orders, with very few exceptions, were given verbally and only to those individuals responsible for executing them. Hitler insisted that each man think only about his task and not be concerned with that of his neighbor. Compartmentalization was formalized in 1940 under General Order No. 1, which forbade government or military workers from knowing more about secret matters than was required for the performance of their duties. The order was posted and communicated to all military personnel, party and government officials (Sereny 1995: 184). The decisions Hitler made with top advisers such as Himmler and Goebbels and with his generals were kept strictly outside his private circle. The atmosphere of secrecy and privileged knowledge that Hitler created not only fostered projective mechanisms, but also made it impossible for the greatest number of his associates to gain a comprehensive picture of Reich activity. As Sereny sees it:

> Underrating Hitler has become a norm, less for historians, of course, than for the media, but it is the media which largely inform the public. It has never been quite clear why so many intelligent people find it more comforting to deprecate Hitler's manic gifts than to view them with awe. But he was by no means only manic. . . . He could also be intelligent and considerate in his more personal relations. Certainly all those who lived around him were keenly aware of his exceptional capacity for compartmentalizing. Hitler would no more have had the ladies of his household – his four secretaries or the young wives of his aides . . . and those of his closest associates, Speer and Brandt – disturbed with war horrors than he would have had the gentlemen of his court, and quite a few of them were indeed gentlemen, involved in his most secret of secrets.
>
> (Sereny 1995: 248)

Hitler's aides, secretaries, and other members of his intimate circle had known nothing of his plans for the civilian population of Eastern Europe and for the Jews of Europe. Those who did know –

Himmler, Heydrich, Goring and later on Goebbels – kept their silence until October of 1943 when Hitler instructed Himmler to inform all top officials of the "final solution."

Speer appears to have internalized this method of compartmentalization as a means of hiding the implications of his own role from himself. At the height of the war, fourteen million workers were engaged in armaments production – the greatest number of whom were prisoners of war and forced laborers brought into Germany from occupied territories. Most of the factories were owned and operated by private industrialists, but the whole was coordinated by Speer's ministry. Speer was in charge of tallying the numbers of workers needed according to the demands of the war effort; but at Nuremberg he claimed no influence upon the methods by which workers were recruited. (Fritz Sauckel, in charge of recruiting labor and technically under Speer's authority was, unlike Speer, executed for his role in organizing slave labor and evacuations of German Jews for extermination.) Speer knew that Jews were being evacuated from Germany, and he fought on numerous occasions for Jewish workers to remain in the country to continue their work in camps. But he never asked himself what happened to those who were exported.

## A slow dawning

Once a life becomes organized along the lines of an archetypal constellation, the perceptual field can be opened and projections withdrawn only by the most violent means. Speer was one of many who were irrevocably invested in the illusion of Hitler's integrity. When asked how they would have responded if they came to know of the atrocities planned and then carried out in the East, Sereny's subjects repeatedly admitted that they would have doubted Hitler's part in them. They were totally convinced that Hitler would not be capable of such atrocities and they would have convinced themselves that it could not be as bad as it sounded, certainly not "if the Führer knew" (Sereny 1995: 248).

By the fall of 1943, Speer's defense against knowing the fate of Europe's Jewish population reached its height. The Allies had already announced that the Reich would be held accountable for its war crimes. In Sereny's view: "Hitler was determined to make sure his supporters were all implicated in the catastrophe he was bringing on Germany" (Sereny 1995: 388). All Reichsleiter and Gauleiter were called to Posen in October. There Himmler debriefed party officials and military representatives on the policy and implementation of the "final solution." At Nuremberg and until his death, Speer claimed that he had not been present for Himmler's speech, despite the fact that the record shows Himmler addressing certain comments to Speer. On the contrary, Speer claims to have been in an informal meeting with Hitler at the time. Neither Speer nor the historians who later wished to expose him as a liar were able to produce definitive evidence one way or another. Whether Speer was present or not, the secret was out, at least among government officials. Nonetheless, Speer tried to convince himself, and did convince the Nuremberg court, that he had been ignorant of the extermination program to the end.

Speer did not, however, remain naive to Hitler's true nature to the end. The turning point came in the winter of 1943 when Hitler's support of Speer began to wane. The atmosphere around Hitler had become tense and filled with intrigue. The war was going badly: the Germans had suffered defeat at Stalingrad, Rommel was losing North Africa; the Allies had won in Tunisia and then landed in Sicily; the battle of Kursk was lost in Russia; carpet bombing had reduced Hamburg to ruins. Hitler had humiliated and dishonored the army, repeatedly ordering that they fight to the last man. Speer, out of sympathy for the generals and loyalty to Hitler, joined several others in a secret plot to undermine Hitler's confidence in the men who were influencing his war policy. The effort failed; instead, Speer became the target of intrigue on the part of Himmler and Bormann, to name a few, who wished to discredit him in the eyes of Hitler. For the first time, Hitler publicly subjected Speer to verbal lashings, rejecting his advice and reminding him that he, Hitler, would decide what was to be done.

At the same time as he was falling into disfavor, Speer heard disturbing reports about conditions in the underground armaments installation called Dora. This labor camp, built by the SS for the production of Wernher von Braun's V-2 rockets, was manned by prisoners from the Buchenwald concentration camp. Speer's ministry bore financial responsibility for the camp, but it fell under the authority of the SS. On 10 December 1943, Speer "forced his way" into the camp to review conditions there. The experience seemed to awaken him to a fuller picture, particularly to his own contribution. The prisoners, who worked 18-hour days, lived in caves with the rockets. It was freezing cold. The caves were equipped with no ventilation, no washing or drinking facilities. Latrines were barrels, standing at each exit from the rows of sleeping surfaces. Prisoners saw daylight only once a week at the Sunday roll call. Of 60,000 men who labored there, only 30,000 survived. "I saw dead men," Speer recalled, "they couldn't hide the truth" (Sereny 1995: 403–5).

As it became increasingly difficult, even unnecessary (given his strained relations with Hitler at this time), to hold off his comprehension of the depth of the regime's criminality, Speer fell seriously ill. A few weeks after his visit to Dora he was hospitalized for exhaustion, depression, and rheumatoid inflammation of his knee. If we interpreted his psychosomatic response to his situation along classical lines, we would surmise his symptoms signified an escape from reality through the dissociation of affect: to defend the ego from unbearable reality, affect is held in the body, deflecting apperception and integration of experience while producing illness. What is interesting about Speer's case, however, is that his illness *followed* rather than obstructed an affective experience. He had been devastated by what he had seen at Dora, and was visibly shaken by Hitler's recent reprimands. Speer, in fact, admitted to Sereny that before this period he had been radically cut off from feeling; but now he was flooded with fear and despair. In light of subsequent events, I believe Speer's illness marked not a radical dissociation of affect but, rather, the *integration* of formerly repressed perceptions and affect. It was a dangerous moment in his journey toward individuation.

Speer's condition soon became critical. He developed a serious pulmonary infarction that caused hemorrhaging. Then, while at the height of danger, Speer had a near-death experience. He found himself hovering above his bed. He observed his body below and the movements of the people who were caring for him. He tells Sereny:

> I have never been so happy in my life. . . . What [the doctor] and the nurses . . . were doing looked like a silent dance to me. The room was so beautiful. . . . I was not alone; there were many figures, all in white and light grey [sic] and there was music. . . . And then somebody said, "Not yet." And I realized they meant I had to go back and I said I didn't want to. But I was told I had to – it was not yet my time.
>
> (Sereny 1995: 416)

Speer's near-death experience defies psychological interpretation, which can only serve to deconstruct a phenomenon that is best left a mystery. Nonetheless, it is clear from the changes in his attitude and actions thereafter that the experience left a profound mark upon his personality. It is as though he had made contact with the Self, for his projections onto Hitler – which bore the marks of a Self-projection – waned after his recovery. Consider the following events.

After his crisis, Speer made remarkable progress toward recovery and was able to leave the hospital to rest at Klessheim in March. There he received Hitler as a visitor. As his recollections of the visit reveal, his projections onto Hitler were receding; his vision of the man he once worshipped was shifting in accord with new knowledge:

> I stood up as he entered the room. He came up to me very quickly holding out his hand. But even as I stretched out mine, I had an extraordinary sense of unfamiliarity. Of course, I hadn't seen him for almost ten weeks, but that wasn't it. It was his face: I looked at it and thought, "My God, how could I never have seen how ugly he is? This broad nose, this sallow skin. Who is this man?" And as these thoughts flashed through my mind, I had a sudden sense of fatigue such as I had not remembered feeling before.
>
> (Sereny 1995: 422)

Speer had not yet given up on Hitler, but his feelings were increasingly marred by ambivalence. By April 1944 Speer admitted to himself that the war was lost, and he became unusually outspoken and defiant in response to Hitler's unfeasible initiatives. In regard to the stream of defiant memoranda that Speer sent Hitler in the latter half of 1944 he states: "I found myself through them. I would never have thought it possible that I would speak so openly, and when I found I could, it gave me an incredible sense of liberation" (Sereny 1995: 426).

Speer had gone so far as to resign over Hitler's orders for construction of huge underground bunkers for airplane construction (the Jager Programme). He was, however, still indispensable to Hitler and so concessions were made and Hitler's favor was reinstated. Not surprisingly, with this return to the security of Hitler's trust came a temporary regression to knowing-and-not-knowing modes of perception. There is one notable example of this regression. In the summer of 1944 Speer's old friend Karl Hanke, Gauleiter of

Lower Silesia, visited him in Berlin. Hanke, appearing confused and speaking "falteringly with many breaks," advised Speer to never, under any circumstances, accept an invitation to visit a concentration camp in Upper Silesia. Speer writes:

> He had seen something there that he was not permitted to describe and moreover could not describe. I did not query him. I did not query Himmler, I did not query Hitler, I did not speak with personal friends. I did not investigate – for I did not want to know what was happening there. Hanke must have been speaking of Auschwitz and then during those few seconds, while Hanke was warning me, the whole responsibility had become reality again. Those seconds were uppermost in my mind when I stated to the International Court at the Nuremberg trial that as an important member of the leadership of the Reich, I had to share the total responsibility for all that had happened. From that moment on, I was inescapably contaminated morally; from fear of discovering something which might have made me turn from my course, I had closed my eyes. . . . I still feel, to this day, responsible for Auschwitz in a wholly personal sense.
>
> (Sereny 1995: 463)

Circumstances, however, prevented Speer from a complete reversion to old illusions. With the summer came the Allied invasions and all hopes for victory were lost. Hitler, maniacally raving against the cowardice of the German army as well as the German people, set his sights first on the destruction of armaments and industry in occupied countries and then followed Stalin's example by issuing his "scorched earth" policy for Germany itself. Speer, finally having differentiated his love for Germany from his love for Hitler, countermanded these orders, one after another. Speer's countermandates were applied against Hitler's orders to destroy industry in Belgium, Holland, France; then industrial installations in Germany, the Balkans; the nickel works in Finland; installations in northern Italy; the oil fields in Hungary and industries in Czechoslovakia. As is well known, Hitler had no concern for the post-war fate of the German population. Speer, on the contrary, foresaw the consequences of Hitler's madness and put his life on the line to prevent further harm to the German people. Of Speer's actions one colleague observed:

He was one of the few public personalities, if indeed not the
only one, who at that point over a period of many months told
Hitler time and again how he saw the true situation and the
extent to which he disagreed with his views. As the year went
on, his one goal become to preserve not only Germany's but
Europe's economic potential for the future.

(Sereny 1995: 460)

It is true that Speer was outspoken with Hitler, but at the same time
he accomplished his purpose by bending the truth. He used his
hard-won awareness of Hitler's madness to his advantage. Playing
into Hitler's delusions, he justified his countermandates by con-
vincing Hitler that Germany's defeat was only temporary and that
industrial and armament sites would be needed as soon as occupied
territories were regained. As a result, the country retained much
needed resources for its post-war recovery.

To be so loved by Hitler was the greatest tragedy of Albert
Speer's life. In him Speer found the hero and protector he had been
seeking since his days as a lonely, passed-over child. While the
collective search for Germany's "One Man" provided an environment for the constellation and sustenance of the possessing archetype, Speer's father complex made him personally susceptible to
compensatory archetypal projections onto a father figure. While
Hitler's faith and favor provided Speer with a long-desired sense of
purpose and well-being, his unconscious fear of losing this fusional
state prolonged a defensive struggle to maintain his idealized image
of the Führer. In Speer's case, a narrowing of the perceptual field
signified the interplay of two intrapsychic mechanisms. First, an
archetypal constellation, as in the case discussed in Chapter 2,
imposed limitations upon the ego's ability to formulate and contextualize perceptions. Second, it appears that eventually ego-
defense mechanisms – repression and denial – *bolstered* the process
for, as time passed, Speer's blindness to his reality became more
active and willful. After his worst fears were realized with his fall
into disfavor, perceptual oversight and self-deception gave way to
illness. With the breakdown of Speer's fusional relationship to
Hitler, Speer's individuation process could proceed. The psychosomatic dimension of his journey initiated the course of his future
development: through his subsequent defiance of Hitler and later
years of reflection, Speer was able to take possession of himself. By
means of illness the ego, seeking its rightful place at the center of

consciousness, made contact with the Self as an *internal* rather than external resource. This realignment of ego and Self appears to have been achieved through a near-death experience that, in the final analysis, signifies a second birth.

# Chapter 4

# The unconscious complex and olfactory messaging

## A case of repetition compulsion

The configuring of experience in conformity with recurring patterns testifies to the role of archetype and complex in character formation. Our best intentions for change cannot stand up against the power of unconscious forces so long as we remain unaware of their nature and presence. Of particular interest to psychoanalysis is the unconscious drive to master an original painful situation by means of its recreation.

Freudian tradition places the *repetition compulsion* among those mechanisms of defense that operate out of the unconscious corridors of the ego. In this formulation, successive but unconscious recreations of an original painful situation defend the ego against the threat of anxiety; it signifies an attempt to free oneself from unpleasure through piecemeal abreaction. Repetition tells a story by means of behavior; abreaction through activity shields the ego against the remembering of an original experience.

This formulation is particularly suited to the phenomenon of repetition originating with concrete events, especially those of a traumatic nature. One striking example of the force of the repetition compulsion in shaping a life is given in Alice Miller's study of Adolf Hitler. Miller traces the roots of Hitler's character back to the cruelty of his father, who subjected young Adolf to countless beatings and other acts of violence. In Miller's view, Hitler projected the aggressions of the father onto his enemies, an aggression that could finally be avenged when he won over the masses and unleashed his murderous fantasies through genocide. His case also demonstrates how, under the right conditions, the operations of the repetition compulsion can seize an entire nation:

It is precisely those events that have never been come to terms with that must seek an outlet in the repetition compulsion. The jubilation characteristic of those who declare war is the expression of the revived hope of finally being able to avenge earlier debasement, and presumably also of relief at finally being permitted to hate and shout. The former child seizes the first opportunity to be active and to break its enforced silence. If the mourning process has not been possible, a person will use the repetition compulsion to try to undo the past and to banish former tragic passivity by means of activity in the present. Since this can't succeed, because of the impossibility of changing the past, wars of this kind do not bring liberation to the aggressor but ultimately lead to catastrophe, even when there are initial victories.

(Miller 1983: 172)

Classical psychoanalysis considers repetitions linked to trauma an abreaction of experience that was originally conscious to the ego. It alternatively attributes repetition to the activity of a repressed impulse that tries to find gratification by resurfacing, only to be once again pushed back by the repressive forces of the ego (Fenichel 1945: 542). But this emphasis upon trauma and impulse control in repetition bypasses important linkages between repetition compulsion and the broader perceptual system.

As we have seen, the unconscious harbors percepts which have never been synthesized and apperceived by the ego as well as memories linked to concrete outer experience. Analysis frequently exposes instances where a life has been significantly shaped by repetition of interpersonal paradigms whose origins lie in diffuse affects linked to unconscious complexes – the contents of which have never been fully conscious. In such a situation the person stands, by means of repetition, on the border between knowing and not-knowing the original condition.

In this chapter we encounter a case of repetition resembling those unconscious interpersonal configurations that Christopher Bollas calls the *unthought known*. As an object relations theorist, Bollas envisages the unthought known as an unspoken paradigm for processing life experience; it is comprised of the rules established between mother and child in the earliest months and years of life. This "densely structured grammar of the ego" is spoken through dreams, parapraxes, phantasies, and especially through transferences; it goes unheard until one submits oneself to psycho-analysis. It is, in short, an unconscious aspect of the ego, the "unrepressed unconscious" (Bollas 1987: 71).

As Bollas brilliantly observes, the intrapsychic and intersubjective experiences of the individual will be shaped according to paradigms known in part, and in part residing in the "shadow of the self." The unthought known is lived in the relational sphere but has never been mentally represented. The object of an analysis in Bollas's formula-tion, is to experience the unthought known in the transference and countertransference so that it might (at least in part) be translated by the analyst into thought.

As in the cases examined by Bollas, my analysand had been sub-ject to patterns of relationship that we finally could attribute to unrepressed unconscious factors. However, those contents related not singly to early object relational patterns, but rather to an interplay of archetypal, cultural, and later developmental factors. She was compelled to reenact a relational dynamic until the unconscious factor was somatically released. As we will see, the compulsion to repeat intensified as the contents moved closer to consciousness. This intensification of repetition served not forget-ting but a finalistic process. Repetition set the ground for cognition through the creation of the associative links prerequisite to release of the complex into consciousness.

The case concerns the academic and relational history of a 28-year-old woman of Swiss descent. She entered analysis after ending a turbulent romance with a man who was 15 years her senior. She claimed to be generally content with her life, but was greatly alarmed by this most recent experience of relationship. She had numerous relationships before this, relationships that invariably ended on her initiative. This time she had tried to save the relation-ship but had been forced to leave her partner after he had become verbally abusive. The experience shattered her hopes for a lasting partnership and her self-respect had been undermined by her lover's accusations. She now had to ask herself what subjective factors lay behind her failure to choose a suitable partner. In her own words:

> In the past I would simply fall into a relationship, it would just happen out of a chemistry and I did not think to ask myself how this love affair compared with those that came before. But after

so many disappointments I am wondering if there is some problem in me, something which is not quite right.

The elusive factor that Lena pursued in her analysis – the thing that was "not quite right" – evaded both of us in the early months of our work together. Lena was professionally successful and highly competent in her social life. A gifted mathematician, she enjoyed the respect of her superiors and colleagues. She seemed constant in her ability to make differentiated, critical evaluations in regard to professional and personal concerns; she enjoyed long-lasting friendships and related responsibly to members of her family. Analysis of her romantic history, however, disclosed a disturbing weakness.

Lena commenced relations with men at a fairly young age. She had never been promiscuous, but she inclined toward intensive, symbiotic entanglements that were invariably short-lived. Initially she would idealize her romantic partner, then break off the relationship after discovering a great disparity between the projected ideal and the actual person. She emphasized the fact that she enjoyed a profound sense of relief each time she left a relationship: "Then I would go through a period where I felt completely content, like I was whole again, self-contained." Lena theorized that her problem lay in her idealization of men, but I sensed a more fundamental problem underlying her relational history. Lena had been repeatedly drawn to men who lacked the capacity to love, who disparaged women and were unable to relate to them as equal partners. These characteristics resided in Lena's current partner. The conflict between the two often coincided with periods of professional achievement for Lena. The greater her success, the more she had been subject to her partner's critical remarks and accusations. As she recalls:

He was becoming increasingly critical of me, and he would imagine that I was thinking terrible things about him, that I was manipulating him, and he would distort even my most innocent remarks, as though I were some kind of monster. Eventually he became openly jealous of my friends, and would consider it a rejection of him whenever I would talk on the phone or go out with others. And he would become enraged when I would dedicate my free time to a project, taking it personally as though I were avoiding him. That's when he blew up and became verbally abusive.

A person's propensity to seek out destructive partnerships may be traced in most cases to the prototype of the parental relationship. However, Lena saw no parallels between her experience and her parents' relational dynamic. Her parents, she claimed, enjoyed a stable and conflict-free marriage. Theirs had been a "love marriage," a union based on love rather than social convention. Her father had, in fact, been "scorned" by his family for marrying outside of his social class. Lena's mother had come from a farming family, while her father's people were of a highly educated, aristocratic line. Lena was their only child.

We explored Lena's feelings toward her parents through the transference and countertransference experience. As with her father, she connected with me intellectually and encouraged me to offer analytic interpretations while deflecting, as with her mother, my affective responses. In the countertransference I suffered anxiety about her relational problems. I further perceived ambivalence in her feelings toward me, and this stimulated within me wistful longings for her acceptance.

By her own admission, Lena was a father's daughter. Her identification with her father extended to her professional ambitions and her unquestionable preference for her father over her mother. She believed that her father loved her "unconditionally," whereas her relations with her mother had always been turbulent. She resented her mother's lack of education and culture, and was somewhat critical of her mother's "primitivism." Lena acknowledged her mother's help in teaching her "feminine arts" such as sewing and crafts, but she resented her mother's tendency to restrict her ambitions for her daughter to marriage and family. Lena wanted to marry someday, but she never aspired to be "just a housewife" like her mother.

Lena's preference for her father was further reflected in her relationships with former teachers and her superiors at work. In the course of her analysis she became aware of her tendency to place herself under the tutelage of powerful, brilliant men who supported her academic work and later helped her to advance professionally. She had been eager to please these paternal figures and allowed them to influence her career choices. She came to discover that she had not yet developed an independent vision of herself as a professional. Instead, she had followed the paths that others had set before her, and her reward was their approval of her progress.

This background opened up the possibility for Lena to consider the problematic side of her attachment to her father and her father's values. She was able to admit that she idealized her father, and had been eager to please him. She attributed this in part to her disappointment in her mother. She eventually realized that her idealization of her father was repeated in her relations with teachers and superiors, and she decided to take a more conscious and independent position in relation to these paternal figures.

I was impressed by Lena's capacity to apply her insights to her professional relations. Her change of attitude was rewarded by enhanced creativity at work and a greater sense of professional satisfaction. Empowered by her insight, she soon decided that her idealization of her father was also the key to her pattern of failed romances, and she was all too ready to hold herself solely accountable for the conflict she suffered in her previous relationship. "After all," she said, "what man could live up to the ideal of my father?" She insisted that she must have been responsible for provoking her lover's rage by holding him to standards that were beyond his reach. Against my advice, Lena returned to her former partner with the intention of working through the difficulties between them.

Jung once said that the force behind our compulsions is not confined to the Shadow, but is also the Anthropos, that inner figure who is the sum of one's potential (Jung 1955: 128). Lena was driven back to the scene of conflict in an effort to find herself within it. The problem in such a repetition, however, is that the triumph can be achieved only with the construction of an associative bridge between the unconscious factor and the consciousness waiting to receive its image. Lena believed she had made the bridge by acknowledging her tendency toward idealization, but she was mistaken. She walked back into a living hell, and her willingness to "work it through" took on masochistic proportions. After two weeks of blissful reunion, the pattern of abuse reappeared. Unfortunately, she took sole responsibility for her lover's rages, and held herself accountable for the "castrations" which he projected onto her.

Lena's situation demonstrates the potential danger imposed by borderland states of knowing. In her desperation to understand her relational problem, to take responsibility and work it through, her judgment was further weakened, and the latent masochism behind her choice of partners was manifest in her return to a destructive situation. Nonetheless, something new was developing, but was made apparent to her only in the form of unconscious effects. I refer to Lena's complaint in this period of her analysis that the smell of her partner had changed. In a discussion with Lena long after this phase of her analysis, she described the situation as follows:

> After my return to the relationship I noticed that M. no longer smelled good to me. In a way, he smelled the same as before, but now his scent was stronger and unpleasant. Before I had loved his smell. When he would be away on business travel, I would pull out a piece of his clothing and bury my nose in it to feel his presence. But now, even though I still loved him, his smell was repulsive to me. I wanted to know why his smell had changed, and I started to watch him to see if he was bathing less frequently or if he had changed his soap. But his habits were the same as when we lived together before. It was as though I had changed somehow, or my nose had changed, but I didn't understand. Then a few months later I noticed that I started to smell different to myself. Later, when I admitted to myself that his view of me was truly distorted, that he had problems and I wasn't responsible, and that he was using me, then I said to myself, "Ha! That's why he smells bad to me!" Somehow I knew the truth, or smelled it, all along!

My protestations against Lena's return to this destructive relationship had failed to impress her; but where I had failed, her sense of smell succeeded. Olfactory "signals" motivated her to keep alert to her situation and to eventually trust her own judgment. She was gradually able to let go of her conception of the problem as a mere idealization issue, and to take a stand against her partner's disparaging behavior. Her perspective was broadening and she began to see her condition in a new light.

In the meantime, Lena's dreams illuminated the relational pattern by portraying the alarming deficits in her development via the *animus imago*. In the early stages of her analysis the contrasexual figures in her dreams displayed, at best, an ambivalent attitude toward her dream-ego. Often Lena would be taunted by a dream lover and occasionally she would find herself under the power of a psychopath or sex offender. Then, as olfactory signals alerted her to the sado-masochistic dimension of her relationship, blatantly destructive *animi* frequented her dreams. Her work around these figures kept her on the brink of seeing something crucial to her development, but she could not quite grasp what "it" was:

I told myself that my current situation was different from the past, because I was working hard on areas of conflict rather than breaking off the relationship. But I carried within a vague feeling of discomfort, like I was living in a state of déjà vu, as though the present had already been and it was all familiar but I wasn't sure how.

Despite her best intentions, Lena's efforts to redeem her relationship failed. She was forced again to leave her partner after a typical argument culminated in a threat of physical violence. Lena vowed never again to demean herself by tolerating the critical judgments of misogynistic men. She composed a portrait of the personality type which she would avoid in future encounters, and decided to refrain from all romantic entanglements for an indefinite period.

Her reflections upon her history and upon her projections onto men bore much analytical fruit during this period, but destructive figures continued to appear in her dreams. Her conscious attitude had changed, but the origins of the *animus* problem continued to evade us. Then, after a one-year respite from relationship, Lena dreamed the following:

I dream that I am sleeping in my apartment and I realize in a dream that my apartment is the car of a train that moves back and forth between two stations, from west to east and back. I awaken and I peer out the window after hearing some commotion from outside. I see a herd of elephants coming from the north, and they run eastward across the land. I go outside. I see two men. One is naked and the other wears a red shirt with black pants. He has dark features and a long scar across his forehead. I ask him what is going on. Then I move to the left where several people are standing, looking out over the edge of a cliff. I want to see what they are looking at. I approach the cliff, but I am overcome by anxiety and I have to crawl to the edge to see what is beyond. It is a sea of boiling water. As I watch it, the boiling stops.

The dream did not make a great impression on Lena until the following evening when she found herself in the presence of a stranger whose features resembled those of the dark man in her dream.

Spotting his familiar face among party guests, Lena approached him. To her amazement she recognized in this stranger not just the dark features of the dream figure but also the distinctive scar across his forehead. She introduced herself to him, and after an hour of animated discussion the two agreed to meet again. A romance was underway in a few short weeks. Unfortunately, when the friendship reached the stage of sexual intimacy Lena discovered, to her great horror, sexual sadism in her new lover. She promptly withdrew from further contact.

This last experience set off a depression which debilitated Lena for several weeks. She was unable to work but kept her analytic appointments. No longer denying that she was subject, by means of repetition, to a powerful unconscious force, she now wondered why she was tricked into relations with this man by dreaming of him before she ever laid eyes on him. She considered herself cursed and grieved her situation with an unprecedented depth of feeling. At the height of her mourning Lena dreamed:

> I am in my parent's house and it is filled with many men whom my father makes me serve, like a housemaid. Then a woman comes, and delivers my piano, which has just been repaired. In the presence of my father, I begin to play the piano, but he makes unpleasant remarks about my playing. I tell him, "If you don't want me to play, why don't you say so directly." He responds, "Fine. I don't want you to play your piano. Why don't you go off and get drunk, like your mother."

Lena puzzled over this scene and claimed her father would never speak to her in this tone. Her father had in fact encouraged her creativity by supporting her musical training throughout her childhood. She also noted that she had never seen her mother drunk; her mother, in fact, rarely consumed alcohol, even on social occasions. But the dream left a lasting impression upon her – an awkward feeling of being subject somehow to her dream-father's punitive attitude.

This dream, alongside others of a similar nature, begged Lena to recognize the link between the father image and the destructive features of the *animus imago*. However, the loving and supportive persona of Lena's personal father shielded her from recognition of the connection. Nonetheless, the lingering effects of the piano dream set the stage for future insight. Several sessions after our discussion of the piano dream, Lena's depression started to lift. She told me that she felt she was very close to understanding something, but she knew she was not quite there. She had, in fact, awakened in the night after dreaming once again of a psychopath. As she was awakening, a voice told her that the "key" to a mystery was given her in the dream:

> I am held captive to the demands of two psychopaths. One controls me by fear and surveillance – he is the dominant one. The other is his partner, a younger and weaker, but perverted character. The dominant one makes me the sexual slave of the second psychopath. I am allowed to go home to my parents. I try to tell my father what is happening, but as soon as I do, I am threatened by the dominant psychopath and pulled back into his orbit. The power of the psychopath makes it impossible for my parents to help me. During numerous scenes, I try to tell others about the problem of the psychopaths, but a surveillance mechanism catches me every time and a mobile phone rings whenever I am "out of line" and I am then either threatened or pulled back to a garage where the psychopaths live. The only exception to this is when I am together with a group of women of my age. The surveillance camera is there but I am angry and less helpless, gaining strength in the company of these women. Later I see myself back in the garage and there is a woman there with me. I am resisting the control of the dominant psychopath, as though something has occurred to weaken him and I have the possibility to escape.

Lena could not fully comprehend the message of her dream, but she felt sure that the younger and weaker psychopath represented her relational pattern while the dominant psychopath stood for a greater unconscious force behind it. During our discussion of this dream I asked Lena for her associations to the garage which appears as the headquarters of the psychopaths. She became tense and she confessed to feeling resistant to her first association. Her father, she stated, frequently worked out of the family garage, where he pursued a hobby of reconstructing the engines of antique automobiles. As a child Lena passed many long hours talking with her father while he worked in the garage. Lena left the hour in a state of extreme discomfort, and she decided to relieve the tension by taking a vigorous swim.

Later that evening I received a telephone call from Lena, who asked if she could see me the next day. She came in a state of remorse and relief, and told me that she had a startling revelation during her swim, a revelation that provided the missing key to her relational pattern. She tearfully explained:

> It was the question about the garage . . . I couldn't get it out of my mind and as I moved in the water I remembered my mother and then it came to me, like lightening, that my father secretly hated her, that he thought she was ignorant, and I was afraid that he would feel the same way about me.

Lena's is the story of all children who grow up under the influence of their parents' shadows. We are all subject to the unconscious conditions of our childhood environment, and these conditions leave their imprint on each individual's destiny. Lena was burdened by components of her father's unconscious personality, qualities she had perceived inwardly. These contents acted as determinants in her intrapsychic world, but could be attributed to no external experience, no concrete memory. By repetition, these contents were given form through outer experience.

In the beginning, the temptation to read Lena's situation along classical lines was great, but had her problem been solely attributed to Oedipal conflict or the appropriation of her mother's *animus*, we would have bypassed the essential dynamic behind the repetition. Lena's idealization of the father and negation of the mother in actuality signified a commingling of archetypal and interpersonal factors. Lena had come to recognize the underside of the civilized and cooperative outer face of her parents' marriage. The apparent necessity for her parents to perpetuate a myth of the triumph of love against great social obstacles left no space in the marriage for open conflict, casting a shadow over the household. A silent battle between Lena's parents wreaked havoc on the development of their daughter's feminine identity. Lena's adoption of her father's interests created the impression, even to her, that she was identified with her father. Yet in truth her efforts to please her father represented her desperate attempt to overcome what she affectively registered as his disdain for the feminine qualities she had appropriated from her mother. She could not accept herself so long as her father's fear of the feminine remained unconscious to her.

Lena's relational pattern further signified her psyche's attempt to address an archetypal conflict of a religious nature. Hidden behind the image of the benevolent father lay a punitive God who, like the patron gods of the ancient Indo-European warriors, robbed the matriarchal deities of their authority, destroyed their shrines, and deprived generations of respect for the feminine face of the creative principle. We might imagine this as the archetypal core of the complex that turns up in Lena's dream of the piano. Here the father forbids her to express the music of her soul, demanding that she instead serve the collective needs of the male group, which have populated her psychic house in disproportionate measure. He further pushes her away, sending her off to join her mother in an oblivion of drunkenness. But by this oblivion she shares the fate of the dismembered god of wine; she is condemned to dissociation and becomes subject to the destructive side of the Eros principle that informs her compulsion.

Nonetheless, Lena's dreams attest to the redemptive purpose of the repetition compulsion. Her mother may have accepted her husband's unspoken devaluation by acquiescing to paternal judgment, but something in Lena rejected this arrangement. While Lena applied her will to giving an alternative shape to her life, an unconscious drive overrode her best intentions by recreating the hidden aspect of the parental paradigm through her attraction to misogynistic men. Lena's pattern reflected back to her the unconscious side of the parental paradigm, a paradigm she had to confront before assuming her true potential as a woman.

We can accept a traditional psychoanalytic interpretation of Lena's situation insofar as repetition reflected her unconscious drive to master a problem originating with childhood experience. Indeed, she wanted to prove her worthiness to a rejecting, critical patriarchy, to overcome what she unconsciously perceived as their hatred of her. Still, we cannot attribute the compulsion to repeat in Lena's case solely to ego defense mechanisms. The subtle process whereby life experience and dream imagery combined for the construction of an associative bridge points to the Self as the choreographer of her transit from diffuse awareness to full recognition of the operative complex. The Self as the architect of her compulsion and its resolution is well illustrated by the striking appearance of a future acquaintance in her dream of the elephants.

The dream of the elephants forecasts Lena's apperception of her situation and depicts the psychic structure that has given her relational pattern its peculiar form. It opens with a portrait of the repetition, by picturing her apartment as the car of a train that continuously moves between two stations, situated respectively in the west and the east. The image shows that the dreamer is caught between opposing points of orientation – one unconscious, the other conscious. The moving herd of elephants offers the possibility that she may gain wisdom – her association to the elephant – by what is to come. The movement of the elephants stirs her to exit her apartment so that she might ask one of two figures what is happening outside. Like Perceval, she must ask a question so that she may learn what lies beyond the barriers to awareness. It is significant that she bypasses the naked man and addresses the man dressed in red and black – the colors of the devil. This is the image of a man whom she would meet the following day. With hindsight we can infer that he embodies the devilish qualities of an *animus* clothed – contaminated – by the shadow of the father.

We generally speak of *animus/a* as an archetype that mediates to the ego the deepest internal contents. Because the internal unknown signifies an "other" to the observing consciousness, this archetype exercises its influence through representations of the sexual counterpart. Whether the *animus/a* mediates perception of the external or internal "other" at any given moment, its actions always imply "two-ness:" a relationship between the I, as a center of consciousness, and a Thou, which is in itself unconscious to the person, even when it is an object of her focused attention. It is this relational aspect of the archetype, I believe, which best represents the essence of the contrasexual *imago*.

The subtly shifting face of the animus reflects back to a woman the development of her femininity over time. The particular face adopted by the animus further reflects her internalization of collective attitudes toward women, womanhood, and femininity as found in both the broader culture and in her childhood environs. This environmentally determined representation of the contrasexual, attached as it were to the *animus* archetype, influences not only a woman's perception of the contrasexual other, but will direct her energically to seek its likeness in the outer world. In this regard, we recognize that the individually acquired *animus representation* stands behind recurring patterns in her relationships with men.

Should those patterns be destructive to a woman's well-being, she must strive toward awareness of the origins of her problem; otherwise restructuring of the *animus imago* cannot be achieved. Because the *animus* image takes shape in a historical-cultural context, the ego must encounter and confront the image with awareness of the developmental dimension. This is the possibility offered to Lena by her dream of the elephants. The dream differentiates the environmentally acquired *animus* representation from the *animus* archetype by placing the dream-ego before two male figures – one clothed, one naked. We can assume that the naked man stands for the archetype of the *animus*, unclothed by the characteristics he would acquire from the interpersonal dimension of her life-journey. In the presence of these two figures, Lena then poses the question that reflects her desire to understand: "what is happening?" She does not wait for the reply to her question, but rather moves toward the left to peer beyond the edge of a cliff. She wants to see what lies beyond with her own eyes. Because the task threatens the established order of her perceptual system, she is overcome by anxiety.

The presence of anxiety tells us that unconscious contents have been activated, and the ego feels endangered. In Freud's view of the repetition compulsion, the ego defends itself against the dread of anxiety by taking flight; the terrifying unconscious content is then displaced by repetitive action, and the ego is saved from the pain of remembering the original experience. According to Jung, anxiety may reflect the ego's unpreparedness to face threatening unconscious drives, but it can also be taken as an invitation to strengthen and extend the conscious attitude. Like the protagonist of folk tale and myth, Lena's response to the threat of anxiety will determine the course of her future development. Significantly, Lena's dream-ego chooses neither heroic fight, nor flight. The dream prescribes an alternative approach to the danger: she crawls to the cliff edge. In doing so, she honors her fear but does not surrender her purpose.

The elusive occurrences depicted in the dream prefigure real events that would follow in the days to come. The dream's prospective function demonstrates the sometimes ruthless means by which the Self achieves its purpose. By featuring a future acquaintance, the dream writes Lena's fate; under its influence, she falls one last time into the old trap. Nonetheless, this last recreation of the destructive paradigm forces her to fully *see* her condition, and the widened perspective to which the dream alludes comes by means of her humiliation. She now accepts her helplessness before the unconscious force mirrored in her compulsion. At the same time, real transformation will be possible only after she makes direct contact with the powerful affects embedded in the unconscious complex-fragments driving the repetitive pattern. The boiling sea that seems to calm itself within her vision brilliantly images these affects.

In retrospect we can accept the repetition as the psyche's attempt to expand ego-consciousness. Repetition serves, not forgetting, but the re-membering of disparate psychic contents that must be given form through experience. The obstacle to knowing in Lena's case was not a defensive rejection of memory, but the absence of associative links prerequisite to cognition. The operations of the elephant dream laid the foundation for the associative bridge that would link the unconscious drive toward resolution of the conflict to the field of ego-consciousness. Lena's comprehension of her situation was dramatically expanded by the romantic encounter that her dream imposed upon her, and her attitude moved from a heroic ego-centered stance to a receptive, mournful surrender to the problem.

During her depressive phase, Lena kept within close proximity to the operative unconscious contents, not through conceptualization, but through her affective response to the experience. In the meantime, the symbolic material showed an intensification of underground psychic activity. Rain seeped through the windows and walls of her home as a recurring dream motif. Then the disapproving and punitive father appeared for the first time. And while Lena could not link the dream-portrait of the father to concrete events, the lingering affect of the dream contributed essential material for the construction of an associative bridge.

With the lifting of depressive feelings, Lena's conceptual capacity could again be utilized. The image of her father's garage as an outpost for the operations of the psychopaths laid the footpath that completed the associative bridge. The affect of the unconscious fragments could be formed into a more coherent complex and attached to the image of "father." Elusive contents were contextualized and synthesized. Consciousness of the formerly unconscious content entered the field of her awareness with the force of an intuition. She had been given the key promised her by the commentating voice of her dream.

The Irish essayist Hubert Butler once said: "We choose some of our experiences and others are forced on us, but they have little meaning till they are related to some central focus of ideas" (1986). Lena's insight into the driving force behind her pattern contributed the focus of ideas around which the meaning of her experience could be organized. Since the archetype escapes our direct comprehension, we can only understand its power to organize experience by tracing its effects back to an original event of a personal nature. Whether or not Lena accurately assessed her father's unspoken attitude is of no real importance. By means of her insight, she was able to reconsider the positive contribution of the maternal principle to her development and to her identity as a woman. Illumining the shadow of the internal father freed her of an unconscious identification with her mother as an object of patriarchal fear and hate. The burden of her compulsion was thus relieved.

In the final analysis, the directive force behind Lena's repetitive pattern cannot merely be attributed to the ego, nor can it be attributed simply to the unconscious effects of a complex operating from the sphere of the personal unconscious. The experience of repetition, itself integral to the process of resolution, was orchestrated by the architect of the dream-work, the Self. And as the striking incidents surrounding the elephant dream reveal, these operations transcended temporal limits. Analytical psychology conceives the Self as a piece of nature. Yet, as Lena's case demonstrates, occurrences we attribute to the Self frequently exceed the known bounds of natural law.

Initially, the known-and-not-known factors behind Lena's interpersonal dynamic could not be translated into consciousness because they were acquired *unconsciously*. Stemming from her father's private, unspoken feeling, these unconscious contents rested within Lena as fragments of affective experience that had not coalesced into a coherent complex. Thus, we can only assume that the archetypal arrangement of these unconscious contents depended upon contributions from the ego-complex by means of associative linking.

Unconscious fragments of experience were translated into a coherent complex (centered around the archetypal image of father) by increments. The means were analytic exploration of events, affects and, largely, being fully present to instances of repetition and weaving the dreamwork into analysis of such instances.

In the final analysis, I believe the cells of Lena's body functioned as a pre-conscious harbor where conscious associations met unconscious fragments over the course of time. It appeared as if midway, through olfactory messages, we witnessed signs that the contents were moving toward coherent complex formation and opening up the possibility of representation. After a final repetition, physical activity released the image into consciousness, as if Lena were birthing an insight after a long labor.

# Part 2

# Chapter 5

# Somatic elements of perception

## The interpersonal origins of awareness

The word *consciousness* always signifies an encounter between two things – self and other, self and world, self and Self. The dyadic constructs that inform our perceptions echo our first awakenings to the world of relationship. The prototype of the mother–child relationship sets the stage for all subsequent forms of knowing.

The perceptual system depends upon the primal relationship for its activation and development. In the infant psyche, the archetypal image of mother can only be attained in relationship to a nurturing caregiver. Perception originates with the child's experience of the mother, for she is the first "world factor" (environmental factor) to stimulate the psychical aspect of archetypal functioning. The inter-personal world of the primal relationship awakens the mother archetype in both infant and mother; as a result, the infant's internal representations of self, mother, and world gradually take shape.

To draw upon Michael Fordham's formulation, we may envision the newborn resting in a "primary self," an archetypal blueprint for development of the psyche-soma. Soon after birth the integral energy of the primary self splits into opposites, constellating the opposing archetypal experiences that are the basis of the develop-ment of consciousness. Thus the conscious/unconscious system grows out of a dynamic process of recurring rhythms whereby the infant's primary self "deintegrates" – opens up toward the environment for satisfaction of archetypal expectations – and then "reintegrates" by turning back into itself for integration of the experience (Fordham 1969).

We may therefore view the infant assimilating and integrating experience by moving between two loci of containment: mother and primary self. As Sidoli observes: "We have to presuppose two arche-typally determined concomitant dynamisms: the deintegration–

reintegration of the primary self, and the to-and-fro of communication within the nursing couple" (Sidoli 2000: 106). This to-and-fro
of communication is analogous to the transcendent function – the
alternation between disparate meanings and affects for symbol
production. As Sidoli points out: "Symbolic creations develop
within the relationship, metaphorically used as a stage where
the interplay of the opposites can be safely experienced" (Sidoli
2000: 106).

We must also consider the baby's experiences of mother's body
and body-self as pre-conscious centers for early fantasy life. The
subjective identity of the individual grows out of the infant's early
experiences of his mother as sometimes indistinct from himself, and
at other times separate. At first the infant is but a small unity of the
total environment or world of the mother; the child's sense of self
grows out of the nursling's physiological and affective experiences
in this containing universe. The infant depends upon the mother
to restore the illusion of unity at times of distress by providing
warmth, rhythm, bodily contact, and the comfort of her voice.
There are times as well when the infant depends upon the mother's
acceptance of their separateness by allowing the infant, for instance,
to fall away from her in the world of sleep.

From these intervals of distress and containment progresses a
differentiation in the infant's psyche – differentiation between its
own body and that first representation of the external world that
is the mother's body. Concurrently, psychical experience will be
differentiated from somatic experience.

By responding adequately to this universal tendency of infants
towards both merging and differentiating, the mother promotes the
archetypal arrangement of representations of mother and maternal
environment within the infant psyche. She simultaneously fosters the growth of the infant's self image which will become the
organizing core of the ego-complex.

Before a coherent psychic representation of the self is achieved,
the infant's experience is largely confined to immediate physiological sensation and unorganized affect. The infant first encounters
herself by means of proprioceptive sensations and her passive recep-
tion of her mother's body. Affective experience will be organized
around feelings of pleasure and displeasure in relation to internal
and external stimuli; the mother image will become attached to
these affective experiences as they are registered in the infant
psyche. The positive and negative valences of the emotions carried

in the mother complex originate with these early experiences of soma as self and mother's ministering body as world.

One of the most significant means by which the infant experiences his body as a separate self is *motility*. The infant becomes increasingly aware of his body responses to internal and external stimuli. His perceptions of self can gradually be systematized in accord with his growing ability to control these body movements. The slow process of differentiation that results depends upon the caretaker's success in regulating the stimuli moving from and toward the infant; infant perceptions of body-self best develop where stimulation is abundant but not overwhelming.

Freud attributed the origins of the defense mechanisms of the ego to this kinesthetic mode of perception (1940). In his view, the construction of a perception apparatus coincides with the development of the apparatus that protects the infant against too intense stimuli and moves her from passivity to activity. Perceptions take place rhythmically under the influence of motor discharge, constituting the first attempt at mastery of the outside world. The process further promotes the differentiation of systems of perception and systems of memory (Freud 1961: 537–49). With this differentiation of perception and memory, the newly formed ego learns to protect itself against too much stimuli by shutting off the function of perception and sinking back into the id – the prototype of the defense mechanisms known as repression and denial, both of which block instinctual demands from perception (Fenichel 1945: 37).

The baby's registration of her own motility, along with her experience of her own body and her mother's body as sometimes unified and sometimes separate, signify the earliest forms of perceptive functioning. It is a pre-symbolic world where the infant, with as yet no means to formulate experience through mental representations, depends upon her body for the expression of affect and excitement. The infant psyche utilizes what Freud envisaged as "thing-presentations" – powerful, unconscious elements expressed in the form of a perceptual or somatic registration of emotional arousal. These thing-presentations must be decoded by the psyche and subsequently carried into action (1915b).

So long as the infant's normal tendencies toward merging and separating are not frustrated, symbolic (semiotic) representations of self, mother, and world will gradually form. The baby starts to invent mother substitutes that provide the warmth, soothing and protective functions of the mother while she is not present (Winnicott

1951: 229–42). Language begins to take over from the more primitive forms of bodily communication. Symbolic communication grows while bodily contact and gestural forms of communication with caregivers slowly diminish. The child becomes a verbal child and learns to compensate his longing for union with the mother by the increase in his sense of individual identity.

Thus the successful development of perceptual functioning hinges on a "good enough" infant–mother interaction. The imagination – the function whereby physiological and affective sensations are psychically transformed into meaningful representations – rests upon these experiences of mother and presupposes the achievement of a nurturing mother *imago*. This maternal *imago* will be contoured in relation to the mother's capacity to modify her baby's physical or psychological pain. If the mother should fail to shield her infant from traumatic overstimulation or exposes him to understimulation, the delicate process of psychic and physiological differentiation may be disturbed. Inadequate maternal responses to infant distress may render the individual incapable of distinguishing self-representation from the representation of the other. The baby may confuse her body with the mother's body, leaving body limits and erogenous zones in a state of undifferentiation. As Joyce McDougall observes:

> Whenever separation and difference are not experienced as psychic acquisitions that enrich and give meaning to instinctual life, they become *feared* as realities that threaten to diminish the self-image or to empty the individual of what is believed to be vital for psychic survival, namely the maintenance of the illusion of fusional oneness with the archaic mother-image of babyhood.
>
> (McDougall 1989: 41)

McDougall describes what Eric Neumann terms the "evocation" of the "Terrible Mother" image. Where infant needs are not adequately met, representations of mother, Self, and world will be negatively conditioned. The predominance of a negative experience of the primal relationship "inundates the ego nucleus, dissolves it or gives it a negative charge" (1973: 74). In particular, where the mother fails to attain an accepting attitude toward the child's body, a negative representation of the Self and exaggerated defense mechanisms of the ego will develop. Stresses upon the ego's attempts to consolidate into an integral unit displace the ego-Self axis in the direction of the Self and threaten the disintegration of personality. Under these circumstances, the "totality function of the Self fails to exert its normal compensatory action." The threat of disintegration expresses itself in the child psyche through an archetypal represen-tation of the devouring, Terrible Mother – a representation that can be located in myriad tales and myths (1973: 50). The developing ego, without recourse to normal compensatory actions of the Self, must defend itself from this threat of annihilation by its own means. The identity then develops out of what Neuman called the "distress ego" or, to use Winnicott's formulation, a "false self."

Part 2 of our study examines the fragility of the distress ego as a motive force behind knowing-and-not-knowing states of awareness in the adult. The cases discussed in succeeding chapters testify to the continual impress of the mother *imago* upon our perceptions of self and world. In particular, disturbances in the maternal *imago* are mirrored by weaknesses in the perceptual system. The synthetic functions will be hampered where the ego is distressed. In such a case, the psychical process of imagination is readily short-circuited; then, the body acts as a field for knowing that which ego-consciousness cannot assimilate. In the next chapter we will see how psychosoma-tism reflects this process and constitutes a primitive form of per-ception that must not be confused with the defense known as repression.

# Chapter 6

# The psyche-soma split

## A case of maternal negligence

I came to know Mary while working in a treatment program for victims of sexual abuse. Mary came to our clinic for family counseling at the request of her 28-year-old daughter. As a child, the daughter had been sexually abused by her maternal uncle. She had come to a point in her therapy where she was ready to inform her mother of her secret childhood trauma.

Over a six-month period we held weekly meetings with Mary and her daughter. Mary claimed to have no previous knowledge of her daughter's misfortune. She was further confused and offended by her daughter's anger toward her, anger that she considered unjust. Our sessions centered upon this stalemate between mother and daughter.

It wasn't that Mary had no sympathy for her daughter. Despite her defensive attitude, she was deeply distressed by her daughter's suffering. Nonetheless she felt she had done her best to protect her child, and she wanted her daughter to understand her own difficulties during the period in question. The following synopsis of Mary's story is extracted from our family therapy sessions and personal interviews, which she later granted in support of this study.

Mary, now a widow, is the mother of two children: her daughter and a younger son. By conventional standards, Mary had been a good caregiver, attentive to her children's health and involved in their education and social activities. She based her marriage and childrearing practices on her image of the ideal family. Mothers, she believed, should be present in the home so that the children never return to an empty house; all meals should be eaten by family members as a unit; money should always be put aside for emergencies; the children must be kept in clean clothes which properly fit them; they should never be witness to disagreements between parents, and so forth.

Mary admittedly organized her vision of the family around themes that were compensatory to the privations of her own childhood. I asked many questions about this childhood during our interviews. "I was raised by my father, a laborer, since I was five," she told me, "and he was always working or out somewhere. Every day I came home to an empty house." And her mother? "Oh, she left us. . . . she had problems with her nerves." I asked Mary to explain. "Well, she had breakdowns. I don't think she was good at family." Good at family? "I don't think she liked married life. She went off and kept house for priests in the city." I asked Mary why she believed her mother did not like family. She responded, "Well, she grew up in an orphanage operated by nuns." The implicit, but unspoken message was that her mother was not interested in sexual relations with her husband and that she was not competent in mothering her young children. In a subsequent interview, Mary told me that her younger brother was just an infant when her mother left the family home. I then asked Mary who had been responsible for the infant's care. "My father took him to a neighbor in the morning," she replied, "and then I watched him after school."

While speaking of her mother's abandonment of her, Mary showed no emotion. When I observed that her mother's departure must have been painful to her, she simply responded, "She visited us sometimes . . . when she wasn't in the hospital." Apparently, her mother's disorder was sometimes so debilitating that she required institutional care. Again I remarked to Mary that these must have been very difficult circumstances for her. "It was OK," she said, "I just didn't like coming home to an empty house."

Under conditions of early abandonment, poverty, and the inordinate pressure of responsibility for self-care and the care of her infant brother, Mary was forced to grow up much too soon. But despite the deficiencies in her childhood environment, she constructed a successful adult life by achieving a stable marriage and raising a family of her own.

In fact, Mary considered her construction and maintenance of a stable family her highest aspiration and greatest achievement. The courage with which she built her family around her ideal became a life-theme among the members of her family, a theme so prevalent in the family ethos that none dared challenge it. For this reason, Mary's daughter – now well into adulthood – could only speak with her mother about her childhood trauma in the presence of supportive counselors.

Thus Mary was confronted with the underside of her family's history in the presence of strangers. During our family sessions, Mary learned how her daughter had been repeatedly molested as a child and how she had silently suffered this ongoing abuse between her fourth and tenth years, often while Mary was at home. Confronted with these facts, Mary was at first incredulous. Soon, however, her denial turned to incomprehension. She repeatedly reminded her daughter that the abusing uncle had behaved properly when she was present. How could she possibly have known under those circumstances? Invariably, her daughter responded, "How could you *not* have known?"

Under the pressure of her daughter's persistent questioning, Mary gradually reconstructed that period in her family's history. Mary and her husband had welcomed Mary's brother into their home after an accident left him physically disabled and unfit for work. Mary remembered that she suffered chronic headaches during this five-year period. The headaches were often so painful that she would be forced to close herself in her bedroom and leave the children under her brother's care.

When we inquired after the cause of Mary's chronic headaches, she seemed particularly unreflective. She simply responded that she has always suffered ailments for which her doctors had no cure and under these circumstances she felt that her daughter was wrong to accuse her of neglecting her duties as a mother. There had been, she insisted, no indication that her brother would bring harm to her children; she had no reason to suspect that he might abuse her trust. When asked if she remembered the changes in her 5-year-old daughter's behavior, if she noticed how frightened and confused the child had become a few short months after her brother's arrival, Mary could only say that those were difficult years in terms of her own health; her daughter, she believed, should take this into account.

In hopes of mapping out Mary's somatic history, I later asked her about the "ailments the doctors could not cure." She reported that she suffered chronic bronchial asthma when she was a child, but that she had enjoyed relatively good health up to the time of her daughter's trauma. Then the chronic headaches began and she suffered acute attacks at least once a week. These headaches subsided when her daughter was about 10 years of age – around the period of her brother's departure. Soon after, however, Mary suffered gastric difficulties; in time these gastric disturbances culminated in an ulcerative colitis, which had to be surgically treated.

In fact, Mary had been subject to several surgeries during her daughter's adolescence. First part of her colon had been removed and later her gallbladder and appendix. Then, when her daughter was preparing to leave home for college, Mary had been stricken with a debilitating rheumatoid arthritis. Consequently, Mary became dependent upon her daughter's care. Luckily, the condition remitted after one year.

Mary saw no connection between her many illnesses and her emotional life. Invariably, her contributions to our discussion of her early and later family history and of her many illnesses centered upon concrete facts and idealizations. Indeed, her memories were organized around the image of the ideal family, an image that she conveyed more in visual than affective terms. This life-theme had encapsulated her daughter, who challenged her mother's self-deception with trepidation.

Without the assistance of Mary's insight into her own psychology, we can only imagine the intrapsychic factors behind her perceptual oversights. We know that the deficits of Mary's childhood had been compensated by her willful construction of an ideal that informed the standards of her mothering. Her five-year oversight of her brother's misuse of her daughter indicates severe impairments in her instinctual and perceptual functions.

Personality is significantly organized by our capacity to know or not know something. A narrowing of perceptual capacity will be found where knowing would elicit affect so violent that it exceeds the ego's capacity for regulation. Something within the psyche acts to keep what could be known on the borders, so that the ego is not confronted with knowledge to which it is not capable of responding.

The life-theme that informed Mary's standard of mothering sheltered her from knowing the truth of her daughter's trauma. It appears that her perceptions of her environment were constricted to the outlines of her childhood imagining of the ideal family. Sensation – impressions from the object world – could not be transformed into ordered perceptions of her daughter's emotional suffering. Cognitive constructs were impermeable to percepts that would challenge her worldview. This continued to play itself out decades after her services as a mother were no longer required. In the words of the daughter, "All she can say is 'I *didn't* know'. She cannot even bring herself to say 'I *should* have known.' "

We can only surmise that the rigidity of Mary's investment in the image of her family's stability further contributed to her daughter's trauma. As a child her daughter felt she could not turn to her parents for help. This, of course, is not uncommon behavior among sexually abused children, as the literature reveals. We might add in this case that by her silence Mary's daughter colluded with Mary's need to sustain her idealizations. Mary's imaging of her ideal family shored up her troubled identity. Not knowing ensured the continuity and integrity of a fragile ego.

I propose that Mary's negligence of her duty to protect her child was due, first and foremost, to an arrested development in the symbolic function of her psyche. We have seen how the normal operations of the perceptual system rest upon the development of a supporting mother *imago*; this hinges upon environmental conditions which allow the baby's natural tendencies toward fusion and differentiation. Mary seemed to struggle to make differentiations in both her thinking and her feeling. In our counseling sessions, she could distinguish her feelings and conceptions from those of her daughter only with assistance from others. The more evident the distinctions between her own memories of the past and those of her daughter, the more defensive she became. Fear permeated the atmosphere, as though some unspeakable anxiety threatened to overcome her.

It seemed that Mary's sense of wholeness rested upon the maintenance of her daughter's persona of well-being. She appeared to be in a state of fusion with her daughter. We may imagine this fusion as a fundamental factor behind her incomprehension of her child's situation. We might also consider the possibility that her rheumatoid arthritis originated with her unspoken fears of separation when it came time for her daughter to leave for university. But we must ask whether or not this kind of self-deception is attributable to repression and denial. I posit that the psychosomatic dimension of Mary's history begs a different interpretation.

Mary refused all knowledge of her psychic suffering. She did, however, recall her *physical sufferings* in great detail. Indeed, she seemed to see herself more as a body-self than as a psychosomatic whole. We may recall how Mary's chronic headaches coincided with the period of her daughter's traumatization. It is as though her body-self registered those environmental factors that had bypassed her conscious apprehension. How are we to understand this?

Current psychoanalytic thinking attributes psychosomatosis to the displacement of affect. A most compelling analysis of this process is offered by Joyce McDougall's study entitled *Theaters of the Body* (1989). McDougall observed from her clinical practice how somatizing patients reveal few neurotic symptoms, as though they maintain a "camouflage of 'pseudonormality' " in order not to think or feel too deeply about inner pain and conflict that might otherwise be experienced as overwhelming and mentally disorganizing. They show a further tendency to be unaware of the connection between their somatic manifestations and psychologically disturbing events in their lives, "much as though perceptions of physical and psychological warning signals were totally ejected from consciousness." McDougall concludes that these perceptions are not denied or repressed and thus unconsciously registered, as occurs in neurotic organizations, but rather all memory of the troubling perceptions is expelled or totally destroyed (McDougal 1989: 27).

She drew this conclusion after working with the more analyzable patients who showed neurotic and characterological organization while at the same time demonstrating temporary somatic manifestations or disturbed perceptual functioning. These patients experienced affect in response to events but destroyed their meaning by somatic manifestations and disturbed perceptual functioning. The process whereby affective responses are destroyed through psychosomatism she calls "psychic deprivation" (1989: 27).

In order to understand how psychosomatism differs from neurotic and psychotic structures, we must consider the role of language. Hysterical and obsessional symptoms are considered substitute formations of repressed thought and affective connections. Neurotic symptomatology then is linked with psychic representation, that is, with meaning. So too, the psychotic patient represents his inner experiences through the use of words and visual imagery. But psychosomatic symptomatology points in a different direction. As McDougall observes:

> With severely somatizing patients there is frequently a pseudonormal communication with the rest of the world . . . in which words, even language itself, tend to be divested of their emotional counterpart, at least in that sector of the personality that is constantly seeking to eliminate recognition of primitive anxieties with psychotic overtones.
>
> (McDougall 1989: 30)

As we have seen, Mary showed this tendency toward "pseudonormal communication" when discussing her daughter's childhood. If we follow McDougall's line of argument, the absence of affective disclosure in Mary's narrative may be traced to a mode of functioning that wards off representation of experiences that threaten to evoke unbearable primitive anxieties. Given her childhood history, it is understandable that such mechanisms would be active in Mary's mothering and in her perceptions of herself as a mother. Her own mother, as we have noted, was mentally disturbed throughout Mary's infancy and childhood. Clearly, her father was not able to compensate for the resulting environmental privations. We can only imagine the nature of the anxieties that impressed themselves upon baby Mary's developing ego.

In the psychoanalytic portrait, psychosomatism signifies the ego's defense against disintegration of the personality. When viewing psychosomatic organization of personality from a Jungian frame, we observe an insufficient constellation of the archetype of perception due to early environmental failures. An individual whose psyche-soma is organized along these lines cannot psychically translate affect into image.

In concert with object relations theorists, Sidoli attributes psychosomatic organization to ego defenses against disintegration. This defense, as she frames it, splits archetypal experience into two halves: it severs the symbolic/psychic from the instinctual/somatic poles of the archetypal image. And while the psychosomatic individual is capable of producing images of a kind, they are detached observers of the images. It appears that when defense operations sever the image from the bodily, instinctual component of the archetype it is emptied of meaning and affective quality (Sidoli 2000: 103–16).

While I am not inclined to attribute this defense operation solely to the ego, Mary's psychosomatosis clearly protected her fragile ego from overwhelming internal and external stimulation. But when attributing psychosomatic organization primarily to defensive operations, one is tempted to view the condition as an intransigent disorder of personality. Might there also be a teleological dimension?

D.W. Winnicott believed there was a finalistic purpose in psychosomatism, viewing it as the means by which the psyche sought repair for the condition he named "the displacement of mind." According to Winnicott, an individual's static conceptual organization of experience signifies the "displacement of mind" in the region of the head. This condition represents an alienation of the individual

from his whole person, as a psyche-soma. In successful development, the "live body is felt by the individual to form the core for the
imaginative self." Distortion in development, however, leads to a
displacement; the mind is felt as something separate from the
psyche. This, he believed, is pathological, for the psyche constitutes
"the imaginative elaboration of somatic parts, feelings, and functions." Further, this imaginative elaboration of soma is not localized
in any one somatic area. On the contrary, a good-enough early
environment results in the experience of psyche as *physical aliveness*
(Winnicott 1949: 243–54).

As is well known, Winnicott traced the origins of mental activity
to the infant's growing capacity to tolerate imperfections in the
early environment. In the earliest weeks of infancy, the instinctual
mother provides an ideally harmonious environment for her infant
– the period of "primal maternal preoccupation." Later, the mother
returns to her normal mode of functioning. Then the baby's
ego-needs and instinctual tensions are not met perfectly. Minor
frustrations produce mental activity in the form of understanding;
the situation produces tolerance in respect of both ego-need and
instinctual tension.

Mind is therefore rooted in the need of the individual "at the core
of the self" for a perfect environment. But where chance events and
erratic behavior by the caretaker impinge too heavily upon the
infant's capacity for tolerance, over-activity of the mental functioning creates an opposition between the mind and the psyche-soma. In
reaction to impingement, the thinking of the individual begins to
take over and organize the caring for the psyche-soma. In health, it
is the function of the environment to do this. Indeed, "in health the
mind does not usurp the environment's function, but makes possible an understanding and eventually a making use of its relative
failure." Where great strain is put on mental functioning, confu-
sional states and inorganic mental defect may ensue. Alternatively,
*mental functioning becomes a thing in itself*, "practically replacing
the good mother and making her unnecessary." The psyche of the
individual is then "seduced" away into this mind from the intimate
relationship that the psyche originally enjoyed with the soma. The
result is a mind-psyche, which is pathological:

> In these terms we can see that one of the aims of *psychosomatic
> illness* is to draw the psyche from the mind back to the original
> intimate association with the soma. It is not sufficient to analyze

the hypochondria of the psychosomatic patient, although this is an essential part of the treatment. One has also to be able to see the *positive value of the somatic disturbance* in its work of counteracting a "seduction" of the psyche into the mind.

(Winnicott 1949: 254)

Winnicott's description of the purpose of psychosomatic suffering implies that the mind, although split off from the body, operates as its own unity. But if we consider the impairments of perceptual functioning that accommodate psychosomatism, we must recognize the striving for psyche-soma unity as a secondary factor in psychosomatic organization. Psychosomatic *organization* of the perceptual system (as differentiated from psychosomatic symptomatology in the neuroses) concerns, first and foremost, the psyche's incapacity to represent and assimilate experience. If we formulate this in terms of the psyche's "longings" we must first look to the developmental deficiencies stemming from the first years of life. As stated earlier, good enough caretaking *promotes* the crucial process whereby psychical and physiological operations become differentiated.

Without recourse to psychical archetypal organization, inner and outer percepts wreak havoc on the psyche-soma. In the healthy psyche, affects are imaginally organized, whether they remain conscious or not. But where archetypal functioning is hampered by an ego whose differentiation functions are impaired, affect remains in a state of archaic, imageless disorganization, and this prevents its release into the perceiving consciousness. Under these conditions, affect fragments are relegated to the body where, as in infancy, all bio-psychic mechanisms of organization originate. We might, therefore say *the body receives, but the consciousness does not perceive* certain experiences. The psyche-soma is in a state of knowing-and-not knowing.

In the adult, this represents a pathological condition, but one that, like all mental suffering, is not without purpose beyond that of defense. I believe the psychosomatic constellation strives, simultaneous with its work in preserving the fragile ego structure, to repair the original fault in the maternal *imago* by reenacting the mother–child dyad. Psychosomatism always calls up an environment of caretaking. In this way, the psyche strives to complete the unfinished work of ego consolidation in the presence of an attending "other." Our next chapter will further explore this dimension of psychosomatic suffering.

# Chapter 7

# Psychosomatics in analysis

## A case of repair
## through regression

The mother *imago* – and the mother–child dyad implicit in the mother complex – continues its crucial role throughout life as the ground of one's security and sense of well-being. Our ability to meet the needs and demands of body and psyche are founded upon early experiences of receiving care, experiences which we daily reenact. Self-nurturing and adaptive functions involve intersections between the mother complex, its archetypal core, and the differentiations between mother and self that comprise ego consciousness. The individual whose archetypal expectations had been adequately met in the early environment is sufficiently capable of meeting the needs of the psyche-soma by drawing upon the supporting *imago* of the good mother.

In Neumann's portrait of the primal relationship, the operations of the mother archetype and the psyche's organization of its functions are set in motion by the infant's first interpersonal experiences. Where environmental factors impede the natural progress of the earliest archetypal arrangements, the compensatory functions of the Self will not develop normally:

> The absence of compensation by the unconscious observed in certain neuroses . . . requires an explanation. In any event it argues against the simplistic thesis that the unconscious, or the total personality, invariable exerts a compensatory action. Such cases of absence of compensation become genetically understandable, however, once we assume that in the crucial phases of psychic development the personal world factor of the archetype (the personal mother or father) must be adequately evoked and activated for normal development, but that in certain patients this personal evocative factor has been absent or

inadequate, so that the archetypal structure of the psyche has been radically disturbed in its functioning.

(Neumann 1973: 82)

We have said that failure in the early environment throws the compensatory function, which the Self provides under normal circumstances, heavily upon the developing ego. Under these conditions, the ego forms as a "distress ego" which impresses the identity with an overwhelming sense of responsibility, low self-esteem and, to use Winnicott's formulation, a "displacement of mind." But paradoxically, this too active and overly responsible ego is not an integral ego. Failures in the primal relationship impede the progress of ego consolidation by inhibiting self–other differentiations. The individual who functions under the impress of a distress ego has not yet been liberated from the psyche's striving to complete this work.

For all of us the process of personality development continues throughout life. But the life of an individual suffering early developmental deficits will be dominantly contoured by an unconscious striving for repair of the perceptual apparatus. In some instances, the personality will be organized along neurotic lines as in, for example, narcissistic personality disorder. Here the individual suffers low-self esteem and shows a tendency toward projection and fusion. Alternatively, the organization may be alexithymic, a condition often accompanied by severe psychosomatism, where one cannot mentally represent emotions. An alternative outcome of archetypal frustrations in childhood would be a neurotic organization with psychosomatic dimensions. This last configuration is found in our next case analysis.

Anna was 30 when she first came to see me. She believed that her marriage was in trouble and she attributed her marital problems to the fact that she did not know herself. Her husband believed that it was time to start a family, but she did not feel ready for motherhood. In fact, her feelings about children were not clear to her. She believed that she *should* want them, but she carried no active interest in them and even, on occasion, found them repulsive.

She further complained of uncertainty about her career path. She had been working with mentally handicapped adults for eight years, but she suffered ongoing difficulties with her superiors whom she believed were overly critical and judgmental. She wanted to change careers but did not have a concept of the kind of work she might enjoy. All she knew was that the demands placed upon her at work were too great, and she suffered feelings of inadequacy when carrying out her duties.

In time I came to recognize how Anna's ambivalence permeated every area of her life, particularly her relationships. She was not at ease when she was left alone; at the same time, she resented the demands that relating placed upon her limited time and energy. She felt that people expected her to take care of them, but that she was given little understanding and sympathy in return. She could not bear her husband's brief absences while he was away on business, but she often felt irritated when he was at home because she could not apply herself to reading or to her exercise regimen in his presence. Anna further complained of the demands her parents placed upon her. She competed with her younger brother for her parents' attention, while simultaneously resenting the interest they took in her life, which she considered invasive.

After months of analytical work we tracked Anna's ambivalence back to her earliest childhood experiences. She was the first of two children. Her mother's pregnancy was unplanned and unwanted. Anna knew the facts of her parent's marriage since she could remember. Her father never loved her mother, but married her to legitimate the pregnancy; he resented his growing family and was openly hostile to her mother; he had affairs and spent many nights away from home. Now, as when she was a child, Anna feared and resented her father. She had always sympathized with her mother's unfortunate marital situation, and she had tried to soothe her mother's pain by continual efforts to be helpful and well behaved.

Fear of her father, however, marred the "idyllic relationship" she enjoyed with her mother as a child. She had been hypersensitive to her mother's moods, and had shared her mother's anxiety in her father's presence. She had clung to her mother's side when her father was in the home, hoping that her presence would ward off some unspeakable catastrophe. This fusional arrangement shaped her image of her father as unloving and withholding. Ultimately, she considered herself responsible for her mother's plight. A feeling of unworthiness pervaded her childhood, and she suffered depressive moods from a very early age.

Anna's history of depression was further accompanied by intermittent bouts of bulimia nervosa. Extremely self-conscious about her body weight, Anna expended an inordinate quantum of energy fighting an unrelenting urge to eat. When the impulse to eat overwhelmed her, she would ward off weight gain by excessive exercise or vomiting. Anna had been partly relieved of this cycle of depression and bulimia after she married. But her relationship with food still disturbed her. She could not attain a relaxed attitude toward eating; nor could she achieve an image of herself as a physically attractive woman.

We know that self-affirmation is not innate, but rather develops out of the interpersonal world of the infant. Because the body is the exclusive scene of the infant's life, the caretaker's acceptance of the body becomes, in Neumann's words, "acceptance as such." Anna attributed the problem of her self-image – which she saw as a problem of her body-image – to the fact that she was unwanted by her father. While this may be true, clinical experience with patients suffering anorexia nervosa and bulimia points largely to conflict between mothers and daughters. While working with Anna, I became especially aware of her habit of splitting her parents into good (mother) and bad (father) objects. She was not always able to differentiate her mother's fears and resentments toward her father from her own feelings and experiences of him. She was quick to criticize her father and quick to defend and even idealize her mother. At the same time, her bulimia betrayed an unconscious conflict with the mother principle: Anna was unable to ingest and internalize maternal nurture. The simultaneous craving for and refusal to ingest food mirrored her ambivalence in relationships.

There were further indications that Anna's problems originated with the mother complex. She frequently complained of strained relations at work, which she attributed to her fears of her (female) superiors. Anna always received favorable written evaluations for her work; she nonetheless felt unappreciated and wrongfully judged by her supervisors. She tended to cast the behavior of her female colleagues and superiors in a persecutory light. She felt intimidated and was unable to speak up or defend herself against what she perceived as unceasing criticism of her work, her appearance, and her personality. Again, Anna compared her relationships with her superiors to her relationship with her father.

Perceptually, Anna resided in a hostile, uncaring world. Consequently, she could not assert herself in her personal relations, nor was she able to defend herself in her work environment. Aggression of any kind, in fact, was intolerable to her. She allotted this important resource no avenue for discharge; instead she was paralyzed by its internalization and its projection out onto the external world.

Anna's father, it seemed, was the first "other" to receive this projection. But the ultimate source of Anna's splitting of mother and father into good and bad objects is likely to have originated with her earliest experience of maternal containment. The infant's experiences of maternal soothing of her affective responses lay the foundation for self-affirmation and for the regulation of affect. In an adequate nurturing environment, the child eventually succeeds in integrating aggressions through the caretaker's acceptance of them and through her efforts to limit and direct affective distress. By internalizing this process the child comes to subordinate aggressive feelings to an integral ego. But where rejection of affective response predominates or, conversely, where the child is spoiled through the caretaker's inability to allow the infant a reasonable measure of frustration, differentiations between self and other will be weak. In essence, a poorly differentiated self-image will be found where the ego fails to regulate disturbing emotions. In such a case, self-care through the constructive interplay of aggression and self-control cannot be achieved.

An individual who has not adequately differentiated herself from her mother will, as in Anna's case, suffer both ambivalence and fear in her relations with others. Anna's psychic fusion with her mother was betrayed by her longing for acceptance, food, and her fear of being left alone. At the same time, the fulfillment of fusional longing threatened to overwhelm her sense of selfhood; the potential loss of her individuality in relationship elicited defensive responses in the form of projection. The "other" then was experienced as invasive, demanding, or in the worst case, persecutory. Despite Anna's positive conscious attitude toward her mother, the mother complex appeared weighted toward the *imago* of the devouring, Terrible Mother. This situation was "known" to Anna, but only by means of her projections onto others. Anna's ambivalence gave further expression to this painful intrapsychic conflict.

Because Anna's aggressions toward her mother were not tolerated in consciousness, they played themselves out through the projection of her hostility onto her supervisors. Early frustrations were internalized as self-hate and she was left with a pervasive feeling of unworthiness. But much of her early wounding eluded mental representation. The still-present anxieties of the infant continued to express themselves through the body-self. She had a long history of psychosomatic illness, which became known to me only after our first year of working together.

At that time, Anna was gaining insight into the problematic side of her lifelong empathy for her mother, and her cravings for food were abating. But as this work of differentiation progressed, she was afflicted with myriad physical maladies. She suffered frequent bouts of fatigue, which sometimes interfered with her work and social obligations. On one occasion she made a dangerous fall down a staircase, leaving her with many bruises and a sprained ankle. This was followed by gastric difficulties and stomach aches.

I was surprised by this sequence of somatic disturbances, because up to this point Anna had exhibited strong affective responses to internal conflicts and her outer life circumstances. Indeed, she wept profusely during our sessions, and expressed joy at the smallest victories in her struggle toward self-knowledge. Yet it was as if we were approaching some unspeakable pain that Anna's tears could not reach. At the same time, Anna stopped dreaming – or at least she could not remember her dreams. These developments suggested an area of personality had been activated which bypassed imaginal functioning.

In her work with somatizing patients, Joyce McDougall discovered a relationship between dreamlessness and psychosomatic organization of personality. She observed in psychosomatic patients a conspicuous lack of dreams and fantasies in circumstances that would normally produce them; it seemed this kind of psychic activity had been replaced by somatic sensations and reactions (McDougall 1989: 104). The phenomenon signifies a disaffectation – the ejection of overwhelming and therefore unrepresentable affect from consciousness.

Describing the course of events from a Jungian standpoint, we observe the occurrence of somatization in its relation to the analytic process. Dream analysis combined with the transference stimulated somatically registered aspects of early experience that had not been subject to archetypal organization. With the onset of psychosomatic symptoms, it *appears* that affective and symbolic activity has receded. Paradoxically, this presentation signifies a situation where affect is far from absent. Instead the individual internally revisits a state where the infant's fledgling perceptual structure had been overwhelmed by an *excess of affect*. When the adult encounters situations that evoke unbearable infant anxieties, primitive mechanisms are activated; excessive affect is then registered somatically. These affects attach neither to the ego complex nor to coherent complexes, but are relegated to the body as affect fragments. Each re-evocation of this primitive mechanism signifies a regression. It is not surprising, therefore, that Anna's psychosomatic disturbances were accompanied by other regressive behaviors.

Anna's depressive feelings and the projection of her aggressions onto others reflected a neurotic level of defense against the mother complex. At this level we had been able to work with repressed affect and representations – hidden factors of personality that could be revealed, examined, and integrated. However, once we reached the somatic level of organization, our work came to a standstill. We both felt helpless. Anna became extremely dependent upon me for reassurance and holding and she seemed to lose all capacity to reflect on her circumstances. My inner response to this situation disturbed me deeply: I fantasized Anna as a suckling who was causing me great pain. In my hostility, I felt compelled to push her away as a kind of forced weaning. I was overwhelmed by feelings of anxiety and self-doubt.

This standstill lasted for several months. As one physical disturbance abated, another would follow. Then a painful and alarming bursitis set into the musculature of Anna's hips. Walking became increasingly difficult until she was forced to use crutches. Her physician assured Anna that her condition was temporary, and he prescribed a course of physiotherapy. Despite her strict adherence to her therapeutic regimen, the condition did not improve as her physician expected. Anna became increasingly fearful that she would not regain full use of her legs. This fear became the sole focus of our work. In the absence of dreams, I hoped that we might gain insight into the situation by approaching it imaginally. We began to speak with Anna's hips and legs, trying to decode the message hidden in her symptoms.

While a detailed study of imaginal approaches to somatic forms of perception falls outside the scope of this study, some basic observations may be of use. First, focused attention of analysand and analyst upon the body – both bodies – promotes regression by replicating the sensually informed temenos of the mother–child dyad. Thus the analyst must know the analysand's ego strengths and weakness and a therapeutic alliance should be well established. When encouraging analysands to give expression to emerging sensations, images, or ideas while focusing upon areas of somatic activity, I am careful not to pressure them to produce organized ideas and images. Indeed, unsymbolized percepts and affects can only be circumambulated by word and image. Often, when the consciousness meets percepts harbored in the body, we are moved to make baby-like sounds and to moan, hum, cry or scream. Images may eventually form out of these percepts, a process analogous to the baby's first stages of language development.

We learn from Fordham's work that our earliest images express archetypes as part of a preconscious system (1955: 89). These primitive imaginal products are not yet differentiated from physical experience. Thus, when working imaginally with pre-symbolic elements in adults, we are returning to pre-conscious centers of awareness in the body. There images can form out of percepts – fragments of experience that may eventually achieve archetypal organization and be released to ego-consciousness.

In imaginal work the analyst holds, witnesses, and reflects on the process. Also, the somatic dimension of the countertransference may be shared with the analysand in language that honors an experience shared, but remains respectfully differentiated.

In addition to the expression and formulation of affects, Anna's imaginal work elicited childhood memories of illness and injury, helping us to reconstruct her long history of bodily forms of knowing. As an infant Anna suffered chronic attacks of colic. She further developed an allergy to milk in the first months of her life. When 4 years old she was treated surgically for appendicitis. She suffered numerous accidents during pre-pubescence and had broken an arm and a collarbone respectively. With adolescence she suffered menstrual irregularity and severe cramping. She had also been hospitalized for pneumonia. The first signs of bulimia appeared in her fourteenth year.

As we reconstructed the psychosomatic dimensions of Anna's childhood, an incident in her working life eventually bore out a pattern of sabotage to healing, a pattern that turned out to be central to her personality organization. After six months of physical agony, the inflammation in Anna's musculature was subsiding. Against her stated interests in a full recovery, Anna volunteered to work overtime, causing her to exceed the limits of physical activity recommended by her physician. She claimed that she felt compelled to work beyond her body's capacity out of fear of judgment by colleagues. Consequently, her condition returned, disabling her as before. She was then forced to consider the depth of her investment in illness and victimhood.

With the passage of time, her condition remitted. Finally her physician released her from physiotherapy and visitation to his practice. Contrary to her own expectations, Anna responded to this good news depressively. Our earlier confrontation with her masochistic attitude at work had set the stage for the realization that she felt abandoned and isolated in the face of health. Her resistance to healing betrayed her desperate need for attention and sympathy. Further analysis unveiled her dependency upon an external caretaking other for a sense of being. The basic functions of the positive maternal *imago* were not fully constellated. The intrapsychic qualities of self-empathy, understanding, and holding were severely lacking. They had to be elicited in the external environment through the creation of stress and bodily disturbance. She came to admit that she felt, without illness or injury, as though she did not truly exist. This revelation marked a turning point in Anna's analysis. Hidden in her bodily suffering was an unspeakable dread of total annihilation. I was now able to recognize her anxiety and she, in turn, was able to verbally express it for the first time.

We may point to two currents in Anna's psychosomatic history. First, injury and illness reflected a reversion to pre-symbolic organization of affective experience. We can only assume that the stresses of the primal environment elicited excessive levels of distress in Anna during her infancy. Overwhelming anxieties exceeded the capacity of the developing perceptual apparatus to organize and represent them. When circumstances in childhood and later life evoked a similar level of affective response, early mechanisms of affect dispersal were triggered. Excess affect, unrepresented and therefore unperceived, was relegated to the body, gaining expression through injury and illness.

Second, psychosomatic manifestations represented efforts on the part of the psyche-soma to redress the deficiencies of the primal relationship. It was clear that Anna's need for sympathy and caretaking were only acceptable to her if she were physically incapacitated; but her psychosomatic suffering signified something more than secondary gain. By reconstructing the mother–child dyad through illness, something in Anna strived to make unimaginable anxiety available for contextualization and symbolization by a sympathetic other. This achieved, unrepresented levels of experience could now be translated to her own perceptual system.

Thus we again take a teleological view of the appearance of psychosomatic symptoms at crucial stages of an analysis. Here I argue a bit with Mara Sidoli, who considered regression to psychosomatism in analysis a resistance to symbolization, a short-circuiting of infantile contents into the body, providing "the last bulwark against integration" (Sidoli 2000: 103). Might we alternatively consider the activity of percept and affect in the body a regression to primitive perceptual mechanisms for the sake of (rather than escape from) symbol production or, more significantly, to shore up deficiencies in the symbolic system itself? Might psychosomatic suffering during analysis signify a crucial aspect of the transference?

This aspect of the transference may be analogous to the developmental stage where the mother "metabolizes" – to use Bion's formulation – the baby's affective experience through regulation and soothing. My countertransference response at this phase of the work with Anna (the feeling to push her from the breast) placed her at risk of re-experiencing maternal failure to organize her distress. This dangerous moment passed when our efforts turned toward decoding body messages through imaginal dialogue with her inflamed muscles.

Anna's case demonstrates the role of the perceptual apparatus in selecting neurotic or somatic forms of defense. Somatic defense often points to areas of experience that have escaped psychical modes of archetypal organization. Affect that is not represented cannot be repressed, but can gain expression through the body-self, as in infancy. The body provides the bridge for transformation of affect fragment into an integral complex. As with the earliest awakenings of imaginative functioning, this process depends for its accomplishment upon an empathic and containing maternal environment.

# Chapter 8

# Building the bridge

## A case of restoration through dyadic imaging

Knowing an experience presupposes the employment of imaginative capacity. With imagination, reality becomes an object of awareness. By means of visual, verbal, somatic, and affective representations the psyche-soma weaves internal and external impressions into meaningful experience. One's sense of being – one's ongoing contact with life energy and meaning – hinges upon the continual recombination of psychic imagery into new patterns. Dynamic imaginative functioning ensures continuity of meaning and vitality. Thus, the promotion of dynamic symbolic functioning is the goal of analysis. In the analytic field, we place our faith in the symbolic power of images for constructing a meaningfully experienced world.

Feelings of self-alienation signify the most global form of knowing-and-not-knowing encountered in the analytical setting. Deadened affect or loss of vitality may encroach at mid-life should established structures and static formulations of meaning leave us in a twilight of awareness. Awakening from a mid-life twilight entails an existential struggle – all preconceptions must be exposed, reassessed, and revised. We must look at where we stand in relation to past hopes, our life-potential, and essential being. Analytical reflection involves, in sum, a confrontation with destiny.

Such a confrontation is possible only where the individual is in possession of an integral ego-complex and a sound identity. Consciousness may then be expanded as one accesses the archetypal energies that give form and meaning to new experience. Our ability to adapt creatively to ever-changing life circumstances, to broaden our identities through experience, rests upon the ego's access to the energic and structural activities of the unconscious.

One's capacity to move forward at mid-life will be severely limited if the ego–Self axis is not fluid, for such a condition imposes

– at the very least – a limited, rigid self-concept. Where the perceptual frame is narrowed by concept-based, directed and causality-oriented thought, we may assume the ego–Self axis has been obstructed by early developmental factors or by excessive ego-orientation over time. The imagination suffers and life becomes stale and static. In such a case, one stands in a borderland of self-knowing, for the depth and breadth of personality have not yet been awakened.

In the right circumstances, surrender to the truth implies surrender to the greater reaches of the personality. But where an individual has suffered limited access to the energies of the unconscious throughout the life span, ego-defenses against the unconscious must be honored. Sudden awareness of shadow contents or precipitous exposure to archetypal energies can expose a fragile ego to disintegrative anxiety. Where the ego–Self axis has been blocked, the ground for knowing the known-and-not-known must first be laid therapeutically, so that insight may enrich rather than threaten identity.

In what follows we observe ground-laying as a feature of the analytic process. Picking up themes from the previous chapters, we will use a picture series to explore the role of soma as a storehouse for the sensed-but-not-perceived. The series, painted by an analysand over the course of two years, portrays the intimate connection between the body field of knowing, the child archetype, and childhood modes of consciousness.

In our case example, picture-making brings the analysand into contact with what Eric Neumann (1973) called "the body-Self." Imaging the child–mother dyad, the analysand revisits the child-ego's field of knowing where body and Self are identical. She unwittingly tracks the ontogenetic development of the ego, depicted through changes in body imagery and containing world. As the work progresses, a relationship between changes in body imagery and developmental shifts in the painter's perceptual system become apparent. Body changes and mother–child dynamics forecast periods of advancement or regression in her capacity to perceive, reflect upon, and accept the circumstances of her life. The case demonstrates how the movement from picture-making to relating within the therapeutic frame builds a bridge across which sensed-but-not-known areas of experience gain meaningful elaboration.

The analysand, whom I will call Lisa, is in the later half of life. When she first came to see me, she told me that she had always lived according to convention, dedicating herself to home and family. Now with her children grown and gone and all obligations to the "world of others" fulfilled, she found herself floating in mid-ocean without a destination. But what troubled her the most was the fact that she did not know who she was anymore. In fact, she had never accessed an identity beyond the outlines of her family relations – first as a daughter to an oppressing and domineering mother, then as a wife and mother.

Lisa, therefore, conceived her analysis as the setting in which she would find her identity. She faced great difficulties, however, because her self-concept had always been externally derived. She could not elaborate an image of her person. In fact, such an elaboration felt dangerous to her, for it had been forbidden by a distressed and dissatisfied mother. She had been told at an early age that she had "no ideas." Emotional expression had not been tolerated. As a result, Lisa's affective and instinctive responses were largely inaccessible to her.

Lisa could not visualize herself as the creator of her future course. She could not discern her values or preferences independent of the viewpoints of others. Once a healthy self-affirming opinion slipped out of her mouth, the forbidding voice of the mother would be activated; Lisa would then retract her assertion. To gain access to her hidden "true self" we had to find means of bypassing collectively derived self-representations as well as the internalized forbidding mother *imago*. Verbal representations of experience could be utilized, but only where they were attached to feelings of loss or desire for life. For the most part, the verbal level had become too entwined with the voice of the deprecating and constrictive mother *imago*.

Where apperception has become static due to collectively imposed formulations of self and world, symbolic forms of expression may be preferable to ideational and verbal modes of communication in the early stages of analysis. To promote her imaginative capacity and access her feelings, Lisa adopted a daily schedule of painting with acrylic colors. Her primary goal was to find a true image of herself as a woman. At first she could not access such an image affectively or visually; but she *could* discern an energic charge around the image of clothing. The shame which had become attached to her awareness of herself as an individual separate from her possessive mother was expressed in her embarrassment over what she called her "superficial" attraction to women's fashion. My role was to affirm and support the pleasure she derived from self-adornment. I encouraged her to paint this motif.

As previously noted, ego-consciousness begins with one's first observations of body motility. Awareness of oneself as a distinct physical being evolves out of movement and the sensation of one's body in relation to mother's body. Thus the body-ego serves as the foundation for all future imagining. In Figure 8.1 Lisa allows herself to imaginally elaborate her body-self as her potential individuality. The myriad ensembles which she portrays express a range of possibility for her future identity. The picture also alludes to her search for identity as a process unfolding in the therapeutic relationship. In the upper left-hand corner two figures, shaded in blue, observe a group of colorfully attired women. For the next year, dyadic relationship would be the central motif in her painting.

In this period, Lisa explored the theme of a mother–child dyad predominantly. She did not aim toward a reconstruction of her early history; in fact, she had little memory of her childhood years. Rather, she used dyadic imagery as a means of making contact with her intrapsychic world and with the affective dimensions of experience that she could not verbally articulate.

The child motif first appeared in a dream occurring at the start of her analysis. In the dream, Lisa encounters a 5-year-old girl in an underground parking garage. She embraces the child and carries her up to the topside world. This tactile encounter with the child – marked by physical warmth and feelings of love and connectedness – left a lasting impression. When embracing the body of the child in her dream Lisa tapped an emotional wellspring long buried in the deep unconscious. In hopes of making this experience more present to her waking self, I suggested she imaginally reenact each detail of the dream while sharing her affective responses with me as she proceeded.

Figure 8.2 represents Lisa's pictorial record of that deeply moving experience. Rather than matching the child image concretely to the figure of her dream, Lisa paints the child as a *newborn* cradled in the vibrant red warmth of the maternal embrace. Significantly, she places the dream-ego's affective connection with the child archetype in the context of the primal relationship.

Much has been said of child archetype as expressed through mythology, literature, dream and art. For example, the image appears recurrently as a symbol of spiritual renewal:

*Figure 8.1* Painting out of her desire to achieve an authentic feminine identity, Lisa portrays two figures (upper left) observing a diverse array of women's apparel

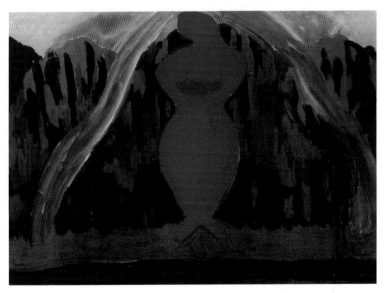

*Figure 8.2* Contacting energies of the child archetype in a dream awakens affect, the foundation of all imagining

*Figure 8.3* A displacement of mind protects Lisa from unbearable anxieties arising in response to an activation of Shadow contents

Figure 8.4 Lisa depicts the positive and negative poles of the mother archetype

*Figure 8.5* A differentiated consciousness grows out of mother's management of the child's early affective experience

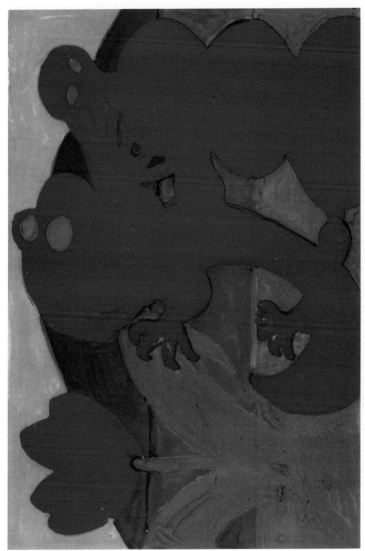

*Figure 8.6* This painting forecasted an imminent regression in the transference

*Figure 8.7* The regression exposes Lisa to formerly disaffected contents from childhood

Figure 8.8 Our ability to contextualize and symbolize affect grows as we internalize the regulatory functions of the capable mother

*Figure 8.9* When the ego is strong-enough, a fall from an idealized, child-centered image of self and world enriches the personality. This is attained through encounter with the Shadow

When I was a child, I spoke like a child, I thought like a child, I reasoned like a child; when I became a man, I gave up childish ways. For now we see in a mirror dimly, but then face to face. Now I know in part; then I shall understand fully, even as I have been fully understood.

(1 Corinthians 13, 11–12)

Jung had much to say about the spiritual function of the child image, but he was especially interested in the compensatory role of this archetype, noting how the child appears where consciousness is one-sided and cut off from the *instinctive* level. Accordingly, Lisa sought contact with the instinctual pole of the archetype through the painting. She could not know herself as a psychosomatic unity so long as she was cut off from her affective life. She intuited the child as its embodiment.

An imaginative encounter with the child archetype activates early modes of knowing, and pushes the body-self as an organ of automorphic development to the forefront. Such an encounter carries the dual function of reconnecting us to our fullest potential for the future while reawakening archaic forms of self-perception. A regressive revisitation to the body-self is of utmost importance for the expansion of awareness. In the child we transcend dichotomies such as past and future, innocence and guilt. The child brings a non-abstractive means of knowing. The energies of this archetype help us break through the limitations of set ways of thinking so that we may start again, body and soul together, and encounter the world afresh. The biases and wounds that close down our vision need no longer obstruct our ability to see. This instinctual aspect of the archetype was intuited by the evangelist when choosing the child as the symbol of spiritual renewal.

The child calls one back to oneself as a bio-psychic unity. In its symbolic functioning, the child is an overarching image of psychosomatic evolution; it points to phylogenetic and ontogenetic processes of development – that which is common to the history of our humanity and to our individuality. It binds us to nature and spirit worlds; it unifies these worlds in our imagining:

The [child] symbol anticipates a nascent state of consciousness. So long as this is not actually in being, the "child" remains a mythological projection which requires religious repetition and renewal by ritual. The Christ Child, for instance, is a religious necessity only so long as the majority of men are incapable of giving psychological reality to the saying: "Except ye become as little children . . .".

(Jung 1951: 168–9)

To hold the child, as Lisa did in her dream, is to hold *undeveloped* emotions and instinctive energies. Once consciousness makes contact with the child symbol, connection with hidden aspects of personality will follow. As we will see, the child links ego-consciousness with elements from the Shadow.

As Figure 8.2 demonstrates, energic contact with the child symbol affectively evokes the primal unity. Implicit in the child archetype is the archetype of the Great Mother, who contains all oppositions. *As soon as consciousness brushes this unity, a splitting of opposites ensues.* Therefore Lisa could not retain the paradisiacal feelings elicited by her dream. On the contrary, oceanic feeling soon gave way to destructive moods and impulses.

When the Shadow is activated, the ego-complex must defend itself against a flood of anger, resentment, and latent anxieties. The regression elicited by Lisa's imaginal work around the child motif naturally triggered early mechanisms of defense against psychic distress. The false (collectively based) self stepped in to defend her fragile ego. As conveyed in Figure 8.3, the mind detached itself from the affective life of her body. Here she depicts her anxiety as a dragon, rising up out of the fire in the left (unconscious) sector of the painting. A figure in gold raises up her hands in a protective stance. Her head is masked in a deep purple hood. The upper body is enveloped in a turquoise sphere, forming a shield against the maw of the dragon.

This reversion to an abstracted and lifeless state could only be tolerated by Lisa for a short period. She soon struggled to once again contact the feelings that her dream had fleetingly awakened. Lisa tried to reawaken symbolic contact with the child image through her painting. At first, she could not break through the wall of negativity that impeded access to the affect trapped in the child-body.

Figure 8.4 depicts this state of entrapment. Through verbal articulation of the condition imaged, Lisa encountered those contents of the mother complex compromising her affective life and her autonomy. Because the child of her dream once awakened her to her own nurturing and containing qualities, that is, to an internal *good* mother, she was now prepared to confront the negative pole of the mother archetype.

In Figure 8.4 the child is held captive in the belly of the Great Mother. Within the womb-shaped field of the mother-realm, two poles of the archetype are imaged. The paradisiacal realm of the mother appears as a green field bearing yellow flowers. The life of the body with its five appendages corresponds to the five-petaled flowers, drawing life from the fertilizing matrix of the field. This same matrix engenders the spirit, the vital instincts, and emotions – the red of the pistils linking these qualities in the symbols of flower and the red, affect-laden child. Standing upon the horizon line is the devouring Spider-Mother, who holds the inflamed child prisoner. The lifelessness of the realm of the Terrible Mother is accentuated by the gray sky behind. As the juxtaposition of these diametrically opposed realms reveals, integration of the dual aspects of the mother *imago* has not been acquired. The energies of the child are caught in the static realm of the unconscious. Lisa cannot access its positive life-giving properties so long as she remains in the grip of the Spider-Mother. Thus, the contours of the child's body show little definition, and she has yet to acquire facial features. This faceless, helpless child, inflamed with suffering, remains encapsulated in the negative pole of the mother archetype. Her disproportionately large arms and hands reach out toward the viewer, indicating the child's profound need for contact, nurture, and freedom to grow into her individuality.

Outside of the womb-world, a pale paper butterfly and grayish-yellow sky allude to the poverty of Lisa's outer life. The sky, lacking depth and articulation of its features, portrays the extent to which the mother complex had robbed her of independent life-conceptions and hampered her capacity to develop her own thinking and feeling attitudes. Basic trust in the unconscious had not been acquired, and rightly so, so long as the Spider-Mother occupied most of the territory below the threshold of consciousness. The energy of the devouring mother exceeds that of the child; thus the mother complex functions like a magnetic field, pulling the child's essential qualities into its underground orbit. Here was a portrait of the intrapsychic process that robbed Lisa of feeling and inhibited her capacity for self-imagining.

After this phase of her analysis, Lisa's imagination extended by increments to her developing ego. In her paintings the child was growing and was repeatedly shown in the company of a handicapped, but present mother. Although the process was unconscious to her, she portrayed the child's body-growth in increments that measured the progressive synthesis of the good and the bad poles of the mother image.

We can see the underlying dynamics in Figure 8.5, where a yellow child, whose features are not yet differentiated, reaches up to her red and attentive mother. The child's instinctive life is still embedded in this red mother, who bends lovingly to a girl who is still more a spirit than an embodied creature. The mother is no longer the devouring mother; still, she is without legs, leaving the child by analogy without her own standing in life. Indeed, the child's affective life will not gain representation until the body-self can internalize the affect lodged in the mother *imago* and thus differentiate from the mother's body. We can surmise by such imaging that Lisa's development was hampered by early failures in affect regulation and the consequent internalization of the personal mother. Amorphous personality features, particularly problems of discernment and differentiation, reveal deficiencies in the mother *imago*. Thus, both child and mother are embedded in the earth with no legs or feet to carry them.

The yellow child suggests the degree to which Lisa's perceptual functioning had been severed from somatic presentations of feeling in early life. In order to repair the rift in her imaginative functioning, Lisa had to endure several painful regressions. Regressive periods where often forecasted by themes in her painting and were manifest in the transference by dependent behaviors and intense anxiety states. These regressive phases were registered in my countertransference in the form of physical pain (bone and muscle cramping) and shared anxiety. Countertransference responses, as is well known, represent a form of knowing-and-not-knowing on the part of the analyst.

The painting presented here as Figure 8.6 prefigured a regression that lasted for several difficult months and which, in retrospect, signified a turning point in Lisa's cognitive development. Here the dyad has devolved to a dramatically archaic level where one embryonic-like figure is fused to another. We can tell by the recurring theme of the arch that we are in the encapsulated world of the mother complex. All former differentiations have dissolved, and both figures are saturated in red. At this point experience cannot be verbally articulated but only sensed somatically, largely by means of anxiety. Painting helped Lisa to withstand and give visual expression to states she had escaped in childhood by means of disaffection. She powerfully communicates this somatic registration of early distress in Figure 8.7. By means of *participation mystique* in the analytic frame and the articulation of her distress in painting, that which was formerly known in soma could now be symbolized.

One month following this regressive phase Lisa showed marked improvements in her ability to articulate feeling and to make differentiated judgments. Concurrently, the mother–child dyad was represented in relational rather than fusional terms. A most striking example is present in Figure 8.8, where mother and child – separated by a small stream – toss a ball back and forth to one another. We may observe significant changes in body imaging and in the quality of Lisa's painting. She has turned from primary poster colors to the more subtle medium of pastels. Most significantly, the mother figure is stylized and elusive, but the child body is mobile with articulated features. The child, dressed in the colors of the earth, receives a red ball that her mother gently tosses to her. The painting suggests that Lisa has gained some distance from the mother complex; at the same time, she receives affective nurture from the good mother *imago*.

The archetype of the child, symbolically manifest in Lisa's initial dream, activated a process that shored up fundamental weaknesses in Lisa's imaginative functioning. This was achieved by her regression to childhood modes of affective experience and perceptual functioning. By moving between fusional and differentiated phases of relating in the analytic frame, she revisited early processes of psychical development in the primal relationship. Early somatic presentations could thereby achieve mental representation through picture-making. Early forms of knowing were further translated into the conceptual frame by means of analytic reflection. All was made possible by the transcendent function and the child archetype.

When Jung speaks of the transcendent function of the symbol, he refers to a process that binds – to use Fordham's formulation – "incompatible opposites of which man appears, not only psychically but also physically, to be composed." When an image operates as symbol:

> . . . the observer gets drawn into his objects, fascinated and even awe-inspired by them, and they evoke in the end his whole conscious activity till he is eventually "thrown together" into a unity. This process is long drawn out and only gradually do the

> symbolical experiences of the wholeness which revive again and again, become more and more real and abiding. Yet what this wholeness is nobody has much idea, it is only known that it is a symbol, and is related to the child images and childlikeness.
>
> (Fordham 1957: 91)

Lisa's longing to gain access to the affective life embodied in the child testifies to the symbolic power of archetypal imagery for transforming known-and-not-known contents into meaningful objects of awareness. The elusive child drew Lisa into the Shadow realm. Her quest for the child necessitated a confrontation with the mother archetype, implicit in the child image. The polarities of the Great Mother had then to be integrated and reconciled in service to Lisa's psychic autonomy.

After three years of picture-making and reflection, Lisa was positioned to confront outdated life-conceptions and arrangements. This reconfiguration of identity and value structures brought about a painful awakening to lost opportunities and undeveloped potentials. The broadening of Lisa's perceptual field signified a fall from Paradise, that primeval twilight state where self and world are sensed but not fully experienced. She unwittingly forecast this fall in Figure 8.9, where she portrays herself as a grown woman who stands in a beautiful orchard. Looking up to the right – in the direction of her future development – she reaches, like Eve, for an apple.

An awakening to the truth of one's inner condition after a long sleep naturally engenders remorse. Such was the suffering of our First Parents as the gates of Paradise closed behind them. Feelings of guilt accompany the fall from paradisiacal twilight into self-consciousness. As agonizing as this can be, the grief roused by such a fall engenders new life, even as it entails the death of an old vision of oneself and of the world. Remorse is linked directly to the discovery of the authentic self. From a mystical viewpoint, remorse is a pathway to the divine:

> Certain sages go so far as to include repentance among the entities created before the world itself. The implication of this remarkable statement is that repentance is a universal, primordial phenomenon; in such a context it has two meanings. One is that it is embedded in the root structure of the world; the other, that before man was created, he was given the possibility

of changing the course of his life. In this latter sense repentance is the highest expression of man's capacity to choose freely – it is a manifestation of the divine in man.

(Steinsaltz 1980: 125)

# Conclusions

By applying the theory of the feeling-toned-complex and the archetypes to our analysis of cases, we have attributed a prospective role
to numerous forms of psychosomatism. The somatic presentations
featured occur in relationship to knowing-and-not-knowing states
of consciousness, where significant areas of experience have yet to
achieve full symbolization.

The range of one's apprehension of experience is determined by
the dynamic operations of the unconscious in relation to collective
and individual factors of personality. Where any one element predominates perceptual operations – whether archetype, complex, or
persona – knowing-and-not-knowing states of consciousness ensue.

We tracked several cases of knowing-and-not-knowing to archetypes and complexes that had overwhelmed the ego's regulatory
functions. Here we redress a bias in psychotherapeutic practice
toward trauma and child abuse. The interplay of identity features
with archetype and complex functioning is fundamental to perception, whether one's ego structure is strong or deficient. Where an
archetype or complex obstructs the synthesis and symbolization of
experience, neurotic symptoms may precede or accompany somatic
presentations.

Perception is a dynamic psychosomatic function where archetypes
attract to themselves somatically registered experience (affects)
alongside contents acquired by consciousness for the continual production of new representations. The archetype therefore organizes
our experiences into meaningful constructs and gives order and
breadth to our imagining of the world. This signifies its positive role
in organizing and animating experience.

So too can the archetype play a limiting role. Archetypes sculpt
perceptions along the lines of intrinsic forms. The selection of

certain contents of experience for production of meaningful constructs presupposes the exclusion of a broad range of external and internal elements. These exclusions circumscribe our understanding and can lead us into conflict with the outside world.

This inhibiting role of the archetype features dramatically in Joseph's story. When one archetype predominates the organization of personality, the consequent narrowing of the perceptual range may hinder adaptation. Constriction of the perceptual field accounts for Joseph's compulsive entrenchment in a heroic behavior pattern. In such a case, the energies of the dominant archetype overshadow the faculty of the will; despite his intentions, Joseph could not step out of his destructive pattern until released from the grip of the archetype.

Because there can be no transformation in the archetype itself, behavioral change hangs upon linkage between the obstructing complex and a fuller range of representations. In Joseph's case, the grip of the archetype was loosened with the construction of an associative bridge to the hero-complex. Through dream work and somatic imagery, Joseph encountered the known-and-not-known inferiority feelings compensated by the complex. Bringing these feelings fully into consciousness, the compensatory hero image was no longer needed.

In a similar vein, we attributed Speer's blindness to Hitler's true character to archetypal constrictions of the architect's perceptual field. From Speer's reflections on an unsatisfying relationship with his father, we surmised the father complex lay behind his personal susceptibility to compensatory archetypal projections. Psychic contamination by the collective projection of the hero image onto Hitler came suddenly but did not loosen its grip for a decade. In our reading, the constraints of the dominating archetype were broken only after Speer's encounter with the Self during a near-death experience.

Lena's story illustrates how circumscription of one's perceptual field may place us at odds with ourselves for, as Jung points out, our unconscious complexes may (by uncanny and mysterious means) perceive things that have eluded consciousness. With the best intentions, Lena could not escape a pattern of repetition so long as the influencing complex remained unconscious to her. The contents of the complex – the "knowing" of which was expressed through interpersonal dynamics – could not be translated into consciousness because they were acquired *unconsciously*, in an affective rather

than explicitly representational context. Thus it appears unsymbolized contents rest in soma as complex fragments, influencing the
psyche-soma through behavior and through somatic phenomena.
With the development of associative links through transference
events and dream analysis, the contents appeared to coalesce into a
coherent complex. As the complex began to cohere, somatic presentations accompanied the expansion of Lena's field of awareness. In
a final "push" via body motility, the complex entered the perceptual
field and the compulsive expression of the known-but-not-known
complex was no longer necessary.

In the course of our interpretation of cases we have questioned
the predominant role of drive theory in attributing perceptual inhibition, perceptual distortion, and psychosomatic phenomena to the
repressive function. As an ego-defense, Joseph's hero-complex succeeded in fending off inferiority feelings, but the constriction of
Joseph's perceptual frame signified perceptual distortion and deflec-
tion of apperception rather than repression of drives or memories.
In such instances, the objective of analysis is the resolution of the
inhibiting complex rather than release of repressed drives. Somatic
image and injury signified the body's involvement by releasing the
operative complex to consciousness. In a similar vein, Lena's compulsion, originating with contents acquired unconsciously, could
not be attributed to recurrent repression of impulse or affect. Rather,
the compulsion appears to reflect the attempts of the psyche-soma
to achieve representation of these contents through behavioral
abreaction.

We attributed the lifelong pattern of psychosomatic suffering
reported by Mary and Anna to developmental stresses in early
life, resulting in weaknesses in the perceptual system. Psyche-soma
splitting – the displacement of the mind from the affective life of the
body – signifies a failure in the early environment, frustrating
the infant's archetypal expectations and producing affect exceeding
the synthetic capacities of the ego. Mind cannot fully symbolize
internal or external experience without access to archetypal operations in the body.

We may also correlate the splitting of psyche-soma with the
formation of a rigid boundary between the conscious/unconscious.
In Chapter 1 we imaged the threshold between conscious and
unconscious as a locus for archetypal organization of memories,
percepts, identity features and affect into mental representations.
Linking psyche-soma splitting to the obstruction of activity at this

threshold, we can conceive how a mind severed from soma produces a limited range of representations and how these images will lack affective vitality commensurate with the severity of the split.

As a pathology, psyche-soma splitting expresses in dramatic form the dualisms residing in the Western psyche. While the differentiation of opposites belongs to the origins of consciousness, the capacity to synthesize and contextualize reflects maturity of vision. We continue to struggle with primitive oppositions of psyche and soma, mind and body inherent in the structure of our language. These implicit dualisms challenge us to describe, and therefore to perceive, the psyche-soma as an integrated physio-spiritual organism. Recognizing that we are collectively in a nascent state of perceiving the individual as a true unity, we peep behind the opposites in hopes of one day apprehending a synthetic image of the psyche-soma.

Experience as well as contemporary scientific research shows us that our subject is, in truth, neither "psyche and soma," nor even "psyche-soma," but rather, an inspirited organism residing within cells distributed throughout the body. Given recent discoveries of the chemistry of memory and affect at the cellular level (Pert 1997: 143), it becomes clear how the language dividing psychic and physiological functions obscures more than it discloses.

In one sense a study like this, emphasizing psyche-soma interconnections, states the obvious. However, through psychoanalytic tradition – particularly drive theory – we have inherited a general tendency to envisage psychosomatic symptoms as a "pushing" of affect or memory *down into* the body. Because this paradigm was born while the Cartesian split greatly influenced Western thought, drive theory is based on assumptions that reinforce our picture of the mind as residing outside of the body. Viewing psychosomatic presentations from a cellular perspective, we might ask, how can one push down into the body what already resides there? In my view, the cases featured in this study suggest a converse movement, that of images "rising up" from the body.

As precursors to insight, the somatic presentations discussed support our imaging the cells of the body as the locus for archetypal transmutation of internal and external sensation into representations. As depicted by *sublimatio* symbolism in alchemy, or in corresponding paradigms of mystical ascent, spirit originates from the body's core and rises "upwards" to the point of apperception. This alternative image has been of tremendous help to my work, for it allows me to place even the most severe psychosomatic presentations within a progressive developmental paradigm.

The spiritual and instinctual poles of the archetypes represent a dynamic unit, severed only by serious deficits in the perceptual function. Where somatic presentations arise, I envisage two possibilities, one within the range of health, the second signifying deficits in the perceptual system itself. First, somatic presentations may signify, to use alchemical symbolism, the heating or grinding action prerequisite to the release of the image – the spiritual face of the archetype – to consciousness. In the event where memory or affective contents have not been organized into a coherent complex, or where a dominating archetypal field obstructs perception, somatic presentations may signal an intensification of this (metaphoric) grinding or heating action for the sake of coagulating the somatically held components needed for the production of representations. The analytic work of constructing an associative bridge promotes linking of these components for completion of the "opus."

Second, somatization on the part of individuals suffering a history of psychosomatic organization signifies a regression to primitive perceptual functioning. Weaknesses in perceptual functioning undoubtedly stem from frustrations of archetypal expectations in the early months of life. Where circumstances trigger forms of affective response that were not contained and contextualized in the primal relationship, the affect is activated somatically. In such a case, translation of primitive affect into mental representations is only possible with repair of the perceptual function. Anna achieved this through regression to the primal relationship in the transference. It appears that Mary unconsciously sought repair through psychological fusion with her daughter.

Revisiting the primal relationship in a therapeutic setting appears the best hope for repair of developmentally based perceptual weakness. When working with psychosomatically organized analysands, analysis of transference and countertransference fantasies is invaluable. I have observed in my countertransference to patients who are organized psychosomatically a recurring fantasy of holding the person like a baby in my arms. Interpretation of this fantasy at an appropriate point in the analysis deepens the work. The analytic container then provides a holding environment where the archetypal needs of the infant *imago* may be met imaginally.

In all cases the interplay between somatic and psychical forms of knowing points to body and psyche as a continuum rather than a duality. This continuum replicates the developmental journey of the infant. The earliest *known* self is a body-self, a bio-psychic unity whose psychical functioning develops out of and becomes conceptually differentiated from its somatic functioning. Still, the adult body remains the locus for regulation, contextualization, and symbolization of experience.

Ego strengths and weaknesses undoubtedly influence this process. As Lisa's story demonstrates, life circumstances may challenge the limits of perceptual functioning and ego integrity. At such times we may return to early modes of functioning in order to redress weaknesses in our imaginative capacity. In a return to the body field of knowing, we recreate the first dawning of self-awareness.

Whether originating with archetype, complex, or developmental deficits, the condition of knowing-and-not-knowing contains its own resolution. Sometimes, knowing-and-not-knowing states produce intensive physiological communications for the sake of constellating the environmental factors needed for healing. At other times, the somatic registration of experience allows the postponement of selected apperceptions until we are ready to receive them. To this end, knowing-and-not-knowing, like repression and denial, may be considered a form of ego defense. Nonetheless, the ultimate *regulator of this phenomenon cannot be said to be the ego*. If an experience has not been represented and released to ego-consciousness, how can the ego cast it away? Who or what anticipates the intolerable nature of selected experiences? Ultimately, the selection of percepts for somatic registration must fall to the Self. Thus the phenomenon of knowing-and-not-knowing points finally to a mystery that transcends psyche-soma, and the laws of time.

# Bibliography

Beres, D. (1960) "Perception, imagination, and reality", *International Journal of Psycho-Analysis,* 61, 4–5: 327–34.

Bollas, C. (1987) *The Shadow of the Object: Psychoanalysis of the Unthought Known,* New York: Columbia University Press.

Butler, H. (1986) *Escape from the Anthill,* Mullingar: Lilliput Press.

Fenichel, O. (1945) *The Psychoanalytic Theory of Neurosis,* New York: Norton.

Fordham, M. (1955) "On the origins of the ego in childhood", *Studien zur analytischen Psychologie C.G. Jung, Bd. I: Beitraege aus Theorie und Praxis, Hrsg. vom C.G. Jung-Institut Zuerich,* Zuerich: Rascher Verlag.

—— (1957) "Reflections on image and symbol", *Journal of Analytical Psychology* 2, 1: 85–92.

—— (1969) *Children as Individuals,* New York: G. P. Putnams Sons.

Freud, S. *The Standard Edition of the Complete Psychological Works of Sigmund Freud,* London: Hogarth Press.

—— (1915a) "Repression", in vol.14.

—— (1915b) "The Unconscious", in vol. 14.

—— (1923) "The Ego and the Id", in vol. 19.

—— (1925) "Negation", in vol. 19.

—— (1940) "Notes from the Mystic Writing Pad", in vol. 21.

—— (1961) *The Interpretation of Dreams,* New York: Wiley.

Hillman, J. (1997) *Myths of the Family,* New York: Sound Horizons.

Jacobi, J. (1959) *Complex Archetype Symbol in the Psychology of C.G. Jung,* Princeton: Princeton University Press.

Jung, C. G. *Collected Works,* Princeton: Bollingen.

—— (1931) "The structure of the psyche", in vol. 8.

—— (1933) "The real and the surreal", in vol. 8.

—— (1935) *The Tavistock Lectures,* in vol. 18.

—— (1936) "Woton", in vol. 10.

—— (1943) "On the psychology of the unconscious", 5th edn, in vol. 7.

—— (1945) "Answers to 'Mishmar' on Adolf Hitler", in vol. 18.

—— (1946) "Epilogue to 'Essays on Contemporary Events' ", in vol. 10.
—— (1948a) "Instinct and the unconscious", in vol. 8.
—— (1948b) "On psychic energy", in vol. 8.
—— (1948c) "A review of the complex theory", in vol. 8.
—— (1951) "The psychology of the child archetype", in vol. 9, I.
—— (1952) "Synchronicity: An acausal connecting principle", in vol. 8.
—— (1954) "On the nature of the psyche", in vol. 8.
—— (1955) *Mysterium Coniunctionis: An Inquiry into the Separation and Synthesis of Psychic Opposites in Alchemy*, in vol. 14.
—— (1961) *Memories, Dreams, Reflections*, New York: Random House.
Kalshed, D. (1996) *The Inner World of Trauma: Archetypal Defenses of the Personal Spirit*, London: Routledge.
Laub, D. and Auerhahn, N. C. (1993) "Knowing and not knowing massive psychic trauma: Forms of traumatic memory", *International Journal of Psycho-Analysis*, 74: 287–302.
McDougall, J. (1989) *Theaters of the Body*, New York: Norton.
Miller, A. (1983) *For Your Own Good: Hidden Cruelty in Child-Rearing and the Roots of Violence* (H. and H. Hannum Trans.) New York: Farrar, Straus, and Giroux.
Neumann, E. (1973) *The Child*, New York: Putnam.
Pert, C. (1997) *Molecules of Emotion*, New York: Scribner.
Ramos, D. (2004) *The Psyche of the Body: A Jungian Approach to Psychosomatics*, Hove: Brunner-Routledge.
Samuels, A. (1985) *Jung and the Post-Jungians*, London: Routledge and Kegan Paul.
Sereny, G. (1995) *Albert Speer: His Battle with Truth*, New York: Alfred A. Knopf.
Sidoli, M. (2000) *When the Body Speaks: The Archetypes in the Body*, P. Blakemore (ed.), London: Routledge.
Steinsaltz, A. (1980) *The Thirteen Petalled Rose*, New York: Basic Books.
von Franz, M.-L. (1980) *Projection and Re-collection in Jungian Psychology*, London: Open Court.
Winnicott, D. (1992) *Through Paediatrics to Psycho-analysis: Collected Papers*, New York: Brunner-Routledge.
—— (1949) "Mind and its relation to the psyche-soma".
—— (1951) "Transitional objects and transitional phenomena".

# Index

abaissement 19–20
abreaction 56–7, 112
abuse: child 4, 80–8, 110; sexual
    80–8; verbal 58, 61, 63
affect 97, 110; access to 104;
    dissociation of 51; primitive 4
aggression: internalization of 92;
    projection of 93, 95; and
    self-control 93
alexithymia 90
ambivalence 91
amnesia 2
analysis: Jungian 1; knowing-and-
    not-knowing in 106;
    psychosomatics in 89–98
animus imago 62–4, 68–9
Anthropos 61
anxiety 69
apperception 10–11, 14, 101
archetypal constellation 54
archetype 6, 110, 115; in character
    formation 56; of the child 4,
    102–4, 107; constellation 4; of
    the Great Mother 104–5, 108; of
    the hero 24–5, 41, 111; and
    identity constriction 24–33; as
    perceptual determinant 9–23;
    poles of 114; role of 5, 110–11
automatism 2
awareness: interpersonal origins of
    75–9

behavior 24; compulsive 32;
    dissociative 2

Beres, David 9–11
Bion, W. 98
bodily injury 1
body: as borderland 3; experience
    of 76–7
body-self 100, 103, 115
Bollas, Christopher 5, 57
Bormann, Martin 50
Braun, Werner von 50
bridge building 99–109
bulimia nervosa 91–2, 96
Butler, Hubert 71

castration: projection of 61
child abuse 4, 80–8, 110
child archetype 4, 102–4, 107
child neglect 3
child–mother relationships 75–8,
    88–9, 100, 102, 107
Churchill, Winston 44
cognition 1, 11
collective shadow 4
communication: pseudonormal
    85–6
complex 6, 115; in character
    formation 56; as perceptual
    determinant 9–23, 111
complex theory 21
conjunctio: ritual 31
conscious 11, 13, 112; intention
    18
consciousness 1–2, 75;
    autohypnotic 19; functions of 15;
    and unconscious 11, 13–15

constellations: archetypal 4
countertransference 60, 96, 106, 114

defense 3, 104; ego 23, 56; mechanisms 2, 16–17, 54, 56; neurotic 98; somatic 98
deficits 115
denial 2, 54, 77, 115
depersonalization 2
depression 64, 70, 91–2, 95, 97; psychotic 18
derealization 2
destiny: confrontation with 99
displacement of mind 90
dissociation 2
distress ego 79, 90
dreamlessness: and psychosomatics 94
dreams 14, 62–5, 70, 102, 111; analysis of 5, 67–70; cessation of 94; imagery of 26–8, 30–1
drive theory 112–13
dyadic imaging 99–109

ego 14, 16–23, 115; and anxiety 69; complex 99, 104; defense 67, 78, 86, 100, 112, 115; development theory of 23; distress 79, 90; and illness 54–5; imposition of affect on 18; integrity 3; and the Self 54–5, 99–100; strengths and weaknesses of 115
exclusion 3
experience: imaginatory 10; limits of 5; perceptual 10; pre-perceptual 10

false self 79
family: idealized 80–1, 83–4
fantasy 14
father: idealization of 60–1, 66; love of 46
feeling-toned complex 5–6, 14, 16–23, 110
Fenichel, O. 17
Fordham, Michael 23, 75, 96, 107–8
free association 16

Freud, Sigmund 3–5, 9, 13–14, 16, 69, 77
fugue states 2

Goebbels, Joseph 37–8, 48–9
Goring, Hermann 42, 49
Great Mother archetype 104–5, 108
grief 108
guilt 108

Hanke, Karl 52–3
hero: archetype of 24–5, 41, 111; complex 24–33, 111
hero-worship 39
Heydrich, Reinhard 49
Hillman, James 4
Himmler, Heinrich 47–50
Hitler, Adolf 3, 34–6, 49–56, 111; projection of paternal aggression 56; seduction of Speer 37–49
homoeroticism 31, 36, 42
human consciousness 9
human responsibility 20

id 17, 77
ideal: projection of 59
idealization: of family 80–1, 83–4; of father 60–1, 66
identity 99–100; archetypal constrictions of 24–33; reconfiguration of 108; search for 101
illness 1, 82–3, 94, 96–7
imagery: dyadic 102; somatic 111; of Terrible Mother 78–9, 93
imaginal system 9–23
imagination 10–11, 24, 99–100
imago: infant 114; mother 78, 84, 88–9, 97, 101, 105–7
individuality: components of 14
infancy: experiences in 12; lack of love in 46, 54
infant–mother relationships see child–mother relationships
injury: resolution through 24–33
intuition 14